GHOSTLY ENCOUNTERS

as experienced by

MARGO WILLIAMS

*To Eileen
With Best Wishes
from
Nick Harrod.*

COACH HOUSE PUBLICATIONS LTD

ISBN No. 1-899-392-106

Published by
Coach House Publications Ltd
The Coach House, School Green Road, Freshwater,
Isle of Wight, PO40 9EB

Printed by
West Island Printers Ltd, Afton Road, Freshwater,
Isle of Wight, PO40 9TT

GHOSTLY ENCOUNTERS

as experienced by

Margo Williams

Research by
Nicholas Hammond

ACKNOWLEDGEMENTS

I should like to thank those who have helped me in my work and especially Nicholas Hammond for researching and writing the historical events in this book, being so supportive and taking part in many releases; I feel this is as much his book as mine. I am the ghost buster, but he is the ghost writer. Thanks, Nick. I should also like to thank Coach House Publications Ltd.

CONTENTS

FOREWORD

For over twenty years Margo Williams has been finding the best documented evidence to confirm the existence of ghosts. Her work has been tested and independently confirmed, even by scientists, and she has been observed by film teams – all of whom have been amazed by the experience; for Margo Williams records the spoken testimony of ghosts and recovers artefacts lost, hidden or buried by the ghost when 'alive'.

It is extraordinary evidence, and even more so to be present as many now have been, to witness this activity. The research confirms the witness accounts of those who have had Near Death Experiences, and so advances the case for the continuation of the personality after the death of the body; but some it seems do not make it through the famous 'tunnel of light' and their physical bodies are in no condition to be reanimated. They are stuck between worlds, earthbound. Ghosts. And what they have to say about the experience is most interesting.

Let them tell you how it is . . .

CHAPTER ONE

THE MOVING HAND WRITES

IN THE past people generally accepted the proposition that there is "life" after death; but in modern times this is rejected by most of the scientific establishment. There is no proof. The problem of course is we only find out for sure after death, by which time it is impossible to wave back to one's fellow sceptics to hail "Halloo over there. Yes, oh yes, I still am. I have survived."

Proof is needed. Faith is not good enough, for that is religion. Yet we must ask ourselves what would be sufficient proof? It is not possible to invite a ghost to take part in a press conference, or bid her rise from the rostrum of a university lecture hall to answer questions. Scientists investigating the paranormal must find other ways to test. Some use electronic gadgetry and wait around in places they believe to be haunted. Others in E.S.P. research take gifted individuals and wire them up to measuring apparatus and perform experiments.

Some investigators take the kind of material supplied by people like me and test it for validity in an attempt to remove "personal" E.S.P. activity from the evidence and so conclude the information could only have been produced by a ghost. Of course there always will be those who refuse to accept it and will find all sorts of contrary explanations, often more improbable than the simple proposition that ghosts exist. But even hardened sceptics have been astonished when witnessing the recovery of a buried artefact on the direction of a ghost who lost it when he or she was alive.

I haven't always had these gifts of being able to see and hear, they have developed over a period of years. I had some psychic ability since childhood but over the course of my life, and especially in the latter third, they have grown stronger and have opened up new and fascinating avenues of wonder.

I could not release ghosts even twenty years ago, and certainly couldn't find the objects they wished me to. At first, and quite unexpectedly, I began to hear from 'free-floating' spirits such as Lizzie while I was doing domestic chores around the house; but she was not the only one. There were others, and when one had finished speaking to me another would visit. I began to suspect they were passing the message around and had formed a queue, for soon I had quite a collection of texts dictated by ghostly souls who seemed simply to want to speak to someone who could hear them. I just listened and wrote what they said.

At first the voices scared me, interrupting me in the middle of what I was doing at the time, and I would have to rush to pick up a pencil and paper. I soon overcame my fear and eventually learned to carry paper and pencil around with me, but this odd behaviour attracted the attention of my husband Walter who became suspicious over the amount of time I spent listening and writing. When I explained what was happening and showed him what I had scribbled down, he shrugged his shoulders and dismissed it as something to do with the menopause; but the voices continued, souls with stories to tell, so I listened.

Most only gave first names, like Lizzie; but when surnames were provided or names of places, then Wally became interested. There were hard facts which could be verified or not. Walter was a scientist and as with all scientists everything had to be proveable. Walter had retired and although his health was poor his mind was active, and investigating the information provided by these 'drop-ins' as I call them gave him something to do.

One spoke of a terrible colliery disaster with miners trapped in a Yorkshire mineshaft; he gave his name as Edward Rose and spoke over a period of two weeks; each time he continued where he'd left off. Walter saw this as an opportunity to prove these voices were some strange disorder of the mind and set about making enquiries. He wrote to the National Coal Board who confirmed there had been a terrible explosion in Swaithe colliery in the year 1875. There was no mention of a man named Rose, but a powder canister belonging to a miner named Edward Rhodes had been recovered and he too had been presumed dead. It was Rhodes, not Rose; the thick Yorkshire accent had obscured the name.

Researchers who investigate so-called drop-in communicators prefer evidence of obscure persons, and the more difficult it is to obtain verifying information strengthens the case, as then it is impossible to have read about the individual. Others followed Edward, many others.

They came day after day, mornings, afternoons, evenings but thankfully not in the night. One famous dead Scottish poet named William Sharp dictated an entire collection of verse and an autobiographical essay, all of which were quickly seized upon by the poet's appreciation society and published as the genuine article, which they are.* The spirits came so often that Wally began to get irritated, complaining they were taking over our life. Indeed it is difficult to give complete attention to a spirit while in the middle of washing one's hair. Wally became a busy man, writing letters here, there and everywhere. He contacted schools and specialised libraries, newspapers and even the Royal Naval College in London to prove the existence of Robert Young, a ship's surgeon on board the *Ardent*.

Robert Young spoke during a morning and an afternoon session, his voice was filled with desperation; and all the while I could almost feel the atmosphere of a lower ship's deck while a sea battle raged all around:

"Men groaning, noise, guns, no fresh air, stench of blood, gun powder. So many men to attend to; shattered human flesh, limbs to amputate, operating room so small... ill equipped on the orlop deck, worse than last time. The British Navy should allocate large quarters for the surgeon to work. So many amputations then, not enough rum for the injured men; mangled flesh which were once healthy sailors...

Femoral artery bleeding, ligatures not holding, men groaning, blood, amputated leg, saw blunted ... needed more help. Damn ship felt like sinking, too many men to see to, too many men injured and dying ... Needed more help; two men to help ... no good. Should have been an Army surgeon. Needed more light, only one lantern to operate by; could not get femoral artery to stop bleeding. Man unconscious thank God."

There was a long pause, then:

"Captain sent for me to repair to his cabin. Always so impeccably attired; I was astonished at his stained uniform and incoherent speech. I had men with terrible injuries to attend to, so was not prepared to hear how well he had done as it was his custom to address me with his victories.

'Robert, I need help,' he said. As he had before only referred to me by my title of surgeon I was perturbed by the use of my christian name. 'The Ardent came through the battle well,' he said. If so many dead men and remains of men in my care was victory, let me form my own opinion sir, I replied. 'Help me Robert, help me.'

I must have more light and another man to clean up. Such

[* *The Wilfion Scripts*. Wilfion Books, Publishers. Paisley, Scotland 1980.]

dim light to amputate by, arms, legs, hands, feet; no end of blood and stench . . . 1797, a year of fighting; not only by sea battle, but the rights of a surgeon for more room and light, for the men wounded for their country. I thought the captain was in his cups but then realised he was in a state of ague, shaking all over. 'Help me Robert, I cannot stop shaking and none of the men must see me.' So it was then I knew I had a weapon sharper than a sword or more powerful than a cannon."

Then the ghostly Robert stopped speaking, and I waited for more; but there was nothing. I waited all morning and still he would not speak for I knew there must be more to come. In the meantime I returned to my normal daily routine and forgot about him.

I was suddenly aware someone was talking and it wasn't Wally. The clock was striking 4 p.m. It was Robert:

"... I can only help you sir if I can have two lanterns from your quarters, rum or strong wine from your stores and two strong men to assist me immediately. I told him to lay down and I would be back with a physic for him, but later. I left taking three bottles of rum and one lantern. The rum helped two dying men into the next world in a more agreeable way than they would have without it.

Battle restarted, more wounded, not enough room ... groaning men everywhere; worked for hours amputating. Trouble with ligatures on blood vessels, legs will not hold me up much longer ... noise, guns, blood. The captain! Forgot his draught. How can he command his ship in battle shaking so? Should have given him my attention more fully. My judgement of the brave gentleman a grave error. I left the wounded men to the care of my helpers and repaired to the captain lest he thought his surgeon forgetful, which I admit I was; to be met halfway by a burly sailor. 'Come quick sir, the captain is wounded.'

When I reached him I knew there was little I could do. Captain Burgess did not survive his grave wounds; the physic I had for him remained in its bottle. Had I got to him before would he have survived the battle? I returned to the men. More and more wounded, more dying, not enough room, not enough of anything. I must write a letter to the Admiralty, but not of the captain's death. Devastation all round me, smoke, guns, noise, screams, blood, legs and death . . . I heard myself screaming for quiet.

Extract from Margo Williams' writings when being spoken to by Robert Young, a ship's surgeon on board the Ardent in 1797.

I kept a journal recording my work, but omitted my forget-fulness regarding the captain's draught or how I refused to treat him unless more rum and lanterns were for my use with the wounded. My journal was incomplete, yet lies with other more important documents that are complete. The battle was long and it was known as Camperdown; so many men and young lads killed. The Admiralty has my journal. It was not published...too many men killed. Not enough light. I could not be blamed for the captain being killed, poor brave man."

Robert spoke no more after that and somehow I guessed his story had finished. It was simple to confirm the battle of Camperdown, which took place in October 1797; but there was little information available locally on the ships that had taken part. Robert had mentioned certain facts, that he was the ship's surgeon on the *Ardent* and that the captain's name was Burgess. Wally contacted Portsmouth Naval Base and they referred him to the Naval College at Greenwich. There a librarian searched and found naval records for the fleet engaged in action against the Dutch and confirmed the *Ardent* had been amongst them – she was a sixty-four gun vessel and suffered heavy losses.

There were casualty lists for each ship and it was clear the *Ardent* suffered the worst of any with 41 dead and 107 wounded; and sure enough the captain was a man by the name of Richard Burgess, killed on that day. Robert had not given his surname, but the Naval College confirmed the *Ardent*'s surgeon was named Robert Young; there was also confirmation of the existence of his journal which can be seen at the Public Records Office. In it there is specific reference

	BRITISH.					DUTCH.			
Ships.	Guns.	Commanders. [* Killed or mortally wounded.]	Killed.	Wounded.	Ships.	Guns.	Commanders. [* Killed or mortally wounded.]	T. Taken. E. Escaped.
Russell . .	74	Capt. Henry Trollope.	..	7	Gelijkheid .	68	Com. H. A. Ruijsch.	T.
Director . .	64	,, William Bligh.	..	7	Beschermer	56	Capt. Hinxt.*	E.
Montagu . .	74	,, John Knight (2).	3	5	Hercules . .	64	Com. Ruijssort.	T.
Veteran . .	64	,, George Gregory.	4	21	Admiraal T. H. De Vries . .}	68	Capt. J. B. Zegers.	T.
Monarch . .	74	(Vice-Adm. Richard Onslow (R). Capt. Edward O'Brien.	36	100			(Vice-Adm. J. W. De Winter.	}T.
Powerful . .	74	,, William O'Brien Drury.	10	78	Vrijheid . .	74	Com. L. W. van Rossum.*	
Monmouth . .	64	(Com. James Walker. (2) actg.	5	22	Staten Generaal .	74	(Rear-Adm. Samuel Storij.	E.
Agincourt . .	64	(Capt. John Williamson (1).	..	..	Wassenaar .	64	Com. A. Holland.	T.
Triumph . .	74	,, William Essington.	29	55	Batavier . .	56	,, Souter.	E.
Venerable . .	74	(Admiral Adam Duncan (B). Capt. William George Fairfax.	15	62	Brutus . . .	74	(Rear-Adm. J. A. Bloijs van Treslong.* Com. Polders.	E.
Ardent . .	64	,, Richard Rundle Burges.*	41	107	Leijden . .	68	,, J. D. Musquetier.	E.
Belford . .	74	,, Sir Thomas Byard.	30	41	Mars, rasé . .	44	,, D. H. Kolff.	E.
Lancaster . .	64	,, John Wells.	3	18	Cerberus . .	68	,, Jacobson.	E.
Belliqueux . .	64	,, John Inglis (2).	25	78	Jupiter . . .	72	(V.-Adm. H. Reijntjes.)	T.
Adamant . .	50	,, William Hotham (2)	..	..	Haarlem . .	68	Com. O. Wiggerts.	T.
Iris . . .	50	,, William Mitchell.	2	21	Alkmaar . .	56	Com. J. W. Krafft.	T.
					Delft . . .	54	Capt. G. Verdooren.	T.
Beaulieu . .	40	,, Francis Fayerman.			Atalante, brig	18	Com. B. Pletz.	E.
Circe . . .	28	,, Peter Halkett.			Heldin . . .	32	,, Dumenil de Lestrille.	E.
Martin . . .	16	(Com. Hon. Charles Paget.			Galathée, brig	18	,, Riverij.	E.
Rose, blr. cutter	10	Lieut. Joseph Brodie.			Minerva . .	24	,, Eijlbracht.	E.
King George, do.	12	,, James Rains.			Ajax, brig . .	18	Lieut. Arkenbout.	E.
Active, do. . .	12	,, J— Hamilton.			Waakzaamheid	24	Com. M. van Nierop.	E.
Diligent, do. .	6	,, T— Dawson.			Embuscade .	36	,, J. Huijs.	T.
Speculator, blr.} .ugger. . .}	8	,, H— Hales.			Daphne, brig .	18	Lieut. Frederiks.	E.
					Monnikendam	44	Com. Th. Lancester.	T.
					Haasje, adv. boat. . . .}	6	Lieut. Hartingsvelt.	E.

Extract from Greenwich naval records showing ships involved in the Battle of Camperdown, and the entry for the Ardent's captain, Richard Burgess.

8

to the work on the femoral artery of one casualty and that Young had to operate for sixteen hours without a mate to assist him in the numerous amputations.

Robert Young was one of many who came to speak during that period. In all there were over thirty cases of 'drop-in' ghosts and Wally had managed to establish full identities for fourteen of them. At least eight of the communicants had died overseas in countries as far apart as the U.S.A., Australia, Sicily and India.

They were from all walks of life, from a humble scullery maid to the wife of a President of America. They were also of widely differing branches of religion: there was a Quaker, a Jew, a Roman Catholic and a member of the Dutch Reformed Church. Most of them were dated in the nineteenth century; the most recent was an Afrikaaner who died in 1965 and the earliest was a Mercer's assistant who described his life around 1770, and a smuggler hung in 1749.

In total there were nearly six hundred scripts, averaging about sixty thousand words. On the strength of this evidence Wally decided to exhibit me. He had concluded that his wife was not having aural hallucinations and that something important was happening here.

There are festivals for paranormal researchers and such events attract all sorts of weird and wonderful people. The Imperial College of Science and Technology was the venue and it was arranged for me to give a talk to the assembled scientists. I am something of a country mouse and found myself petrified at the moment of standing up in front of all the boffins.

I was both fascinated and slightly sickened to see a diagram of my brain scrawled across a blackboard, and some professor armed with a chalkstick and equations of Quantum Mechanics which he assured me could explain the abilities I enjoyed. I did not understand a word of it and by the time he had finished his hour's discussion of the mechanics of my brain, I felt I no longer possessed one. Many learned men and women expressed great interest in my work and several spoke with Wally about arrangements to get me in their laboratories for experiments.

*   *   *

It was in the winter of 1978 that I stumbled across the phenomenon of ghosts as most people think of them; that is to say, spirits who haunt particular locations and whose activity scares the living who encounter them. I had been pondering on whether to go to the laboratories and be wired up to the machinery for tests. Wally seemed most enthusiastic; but when I asked him what they would do to me he shrugged his shoulders and spoke about measuring brain activity and such like. He could tell I was not keen, and when I asked what it would prove he said he did not know for sure. It was just scientific research.

One afternoon during this period I walked the cliff paths near my home; from time to time I had met Mrs Jenny Gibbons as we walked our dogs, but that day she stopped to talk and for some reason she decided to tell me how she could sense whether an animal was friendly or not and believed she was psychic in some way. Perhaps it was the difficult decision I had to make concerning the experiments but I told her of my own gifts and we set about talking of psychicism.

It was two weeks later when I saw her again. She was hammering on the door of my house and seemed most agitated. "Will you come to Appledurcombe?" Her big blue eyes were wide with excitement. "There's something screaming. I think someone's whipping a horse!"

I looked blankly at her and asked what I could possibly do from here if someone was whipping a horse up at Appledurcombe. "I'm not the R.S.P.C.A."

Jenny shook her head and spoke almost breathlessly. "It's a ghost. I'm sure you can help."

"I've never had anything to do with ghosts."

Jenny was almost pleading with me. "You must try. It's urgent."

I told her perhaps I'd take a look next week, for we didn't have a car.

"No. No. Now! I'll take you in mine."

By this time Wally had come to the door and I explained as best I could what was going on. He seemed happy enough to go see, he had nothing better to do and said he fancied a drive.

The closer we came to the old ruined house of Appledurcombe the more excited Jenny became. She explained how she had heard screaming in the *porte cochère*, the grand covered entranceway at the back of the house. I had taken pencil and paper, knowing the experience of the "drop-ins", and as we wandered around the area I found myself being drawn to an old stone mounting block, then I couldn't help but stumble backwards against a wall needing something to support me. Wally watched while Jenny pulled out a camera and took photographs; she had it right, something was being whipped. But it wasn't a horse. It was a girl; and at that moment I discovered I could also hear the voices of ghosts.

First it was screaming, terrible frantic screaming; then the voice:

"Richard beat me with his riding crop when I tells him I am with child, his babe. Carried the whip marks to my dying day. My baby was a boy, it's a wonder he lived after such a beating. I pleaded for mercy."

There was a long pause. Then:

"Oh Richard, I a poor maid loved you so much. You took my body many times. My name is Mary Target. Please take me to Richard's tomb in the church."

I waited, but there was no more, though I felt the presence around me. There was no doubt the ghost was still about. My companions were astonished when I read to them what I had written as dictation, and there was some discussion over her last words. Wally was sure the ghost must have something to do with the Worsley family whose home Appledurcombe had been for centuries; as for the church, that would have to be Godshill, for there can be found the family tombs.

Jenny was overjoyed, for that afternoon proved to her beyond doubt that what she had heard was not of the imagination; for like me she had known self-doubt about such mystical experiences. As we all stood in Godshill church some time later, before the Worsley memorials, Mary Target spoke again, and for the last time:

"I have haunted the place where you beat me, Richard. I am nearer you at last and am free."

Any doubts I may have about the ghostly confessions are usually dispelled when their identities are confirmed. Wally set about finding who Mary Targett might have been, and the history of the Worsley family is well documented. Amongst all the text he came across a key reference: "Thomas Worsley of Chale was a bastard begotten by Mr Richard Worsley of Appledurcombe on the body of Urie Targett's daughter who dwelt at Watchingwell, and this maid was his dairymaid, and a good handsome wench."*

From that day onward I decided to devote my life to helping these poor trapped souls wherever I may find them.

[*See *The Oglander Diaries. A Royalist's Notebook. The Commonplace Book of Sir John Oglander, Kt, of Nunwell.* Constable & Co. 1936.]

CHAPTER TWO

THE SWEETEST BED OF ALL

OLD AND ruined mansions, a notorious titled family and crimes of passion; what more typical ingredients could there be for a haunting? Several hauntings in fact. For some residents it seems the past cannot be forgotten and even the living cannot escape the history of their houses.

Within the shores of this garden isle can be found the history of Britain. To the west there are the prehistoric barrows and standing stones of the early inhabitants, from the time when the floods swept away homelands and carried people to new shores. In time the Celts too revered these stones and the great Needle rocks; they called this island Ynis Wyth and some say honoured here the heavenly Alwen, she who presides over love and beauty.*

Beneath the soil can be found the sedimented layers of conquerors' bones and homes and temples, long since ploughed under or built over. The Romans came in the year 43 AD with fifty-thousand men armed with short swords, shields and hob-nailed sandals. Where once the pole and wattle huts stood in circles in the forest clearings they built villas of stone and roads between them; around the villas they planted orchards and laid gardens and found the soil good for growing fruit trees. Yet by the 400s they were looking homeward, collecting up what treasures they possessed and burying what they could not carry as the Empire foundered and Jutes and Saxons arrived in Britain.

In the year 530 Cerdic and Cynric crashed through the under-growth and slaughtered the community at Carisbrooke and took the Island; when nephews Stuf and Wihtgar inherited the lot, some say the Island won its name of Wight.

The new rulers made encampments and as the Roman tiles broke and mortar crumbled, new structures were built with the stone, and for a short while the old temples were used for the worship of Thor and Odin, Freyer and runestones. Through Saxon and Viking times and into the age of the Normans, estates expanded as the land and its great houses passed from conqueror to conqueror; as the families

[*A Ring Of Magic Islands. Sybil and Stephen Leek. American Photographic Book Publishing Co. 1975.]

made their homes the houses were extended or destroyed according to taste. Walls and paintwork may have come and gone but, it seems, some residents have not been so lucky.

Margaret Pakenham was not my first case of releasing a ghost from a haunting, but she was certainly one of the oldest to date. She was found haunting the grounds of a beautiful country manor house in the village of Gatcombe. The village has changed little over recent years, indeed the world of progress has largely passed it by in its picturesque position at the foot of a chalk gorge. Some might call Gatcombe 'sleepy', for it has no school, no shop and no inn to relieve the villagers. Its chief buildings are the manor house and church which stands next door.

The house is a pretty three-storey, ivy-covered box with plenty of windows. It stands on the site of an older residence; behind rise the forests of the downs, and in front the lawns slope gently towards the lake. It is truly a lovely setting. Although there is a main entrance and driveway to the house, it can best be seen from the grounds of the churchyard. I was accompanied by Wally and it was an unusually mild autumn morning when we arrived at the iron gateway to the church. Beside the wall I saw a tall crab apple tree bursting with yellow fruit and dripping with moisture from the mists. As we walked down the gravel path, ahead the rising sun's rays were spreading through the archway of leaves of a chestnut tree; the yellowing leaves and mist and rays and moisture made it look as if nature itself was dripping with gold.

Wally busied himself by walking around the churchyard while I waited. He was reading the tombstones and I was wondering where the ghost might be. I never know for sure beforehand exactly where the ghost is, who it might be or from what era. This all becomes clear when he or she speaks. I had a feeling the ghost was not in the churchyard but in the park on the other side of the hedge. The house is occupied and I hoped the ghost could move close enough for me to hear. As always I carried with me a pencil and some paper, and so I waited and listened. The ground was damp and I had nowhere to sit, so I slowly walked along beside the hedge and found myself being drawn towards the lake. Suddenly there was a terrible sensation of being drawn backwards, ever backwards, further and further. Then a voice.

"I prithee forgive me as I take the liberty of addressing someone who listens and hears. I find I conducted myself perfidiously and cruelly wronged my sister Elizabeth, a jewel among knaves. I strayed from my birth and breeding. Margaret is my name.

It was my bounden duty to obey my sire and I became the spouse of John while Elizabeth wed Dudley whom I trusted not. The face of an angel, the heart of a knave. The manors our sire left entrusted to our care. Then strife between sisters, my heart dwelt with the devil.

I entreat thee to write these words with love in thy heart for an erring wife and sister who enshrouded herself in a cloak of hatred and envy. I submit my voice to thine ears, syllables of truth thou hearest. Elizabeth and Dudley, so proud of their estates, I wronged. My passionate devotion for a serving man had dishonoured me in my spouse's eyes, yet I forgot God.

A letter penned as if by my sister was enough to sow the seeds of discontent in the heart of her husband, a knave himself who dallied with the wenches. My sister sick with worry while I am vainly blinded by false words of love.

My imperious flood of words I trust disturb thee not. The name of Pakenham to be dishonoured could ne'er be, the name of Dudley troubled me not. So the letter was penned as if by my

Gatcombe House.

14

fair sister. Now I seek her forgiveness. I look for her and find her not. This house changed over the years, timeless, meaningless years, but still I seek her. Help me I prithee, to escape this house that is my prison, my dungeon, my cage."

And the voice was gone. Wally had to hold me up as I was near to fainting and this never normally happens with releasing ghosts. Wally shook me and was asking what had happened and I described the awful feeling of falling backwards, and then I unclenched my fingers from the paper which with some relief I saw had writing on. I could barely see it to read as for some reason the encounter had left me feeling weak and most unwell.

I managed to read the message to Wally and guessed there was more to come, although I didn't much relish the prospect of doing that again. It was most horrible and uncomfortable. As the ground was wet Wally led me inside the church to sit down. The church of Saint Olave is warm, for it has a powerful central heating system which in mild weather creates something of a tropical feel. The effect made my head swim all the more, but somehow as we both sat quietly I managed to regain some composure and again I felt the ghostly presence. She had followed me inside.

"Welcome to thee mistress Margaret from the Margaret who once dwelt in the manor. Fortune smiles upon me that thou shouldst visit here. I entreated thee to come and to be prayed for is what this evil woman needed. I see Elizabeth who I wronged so cruelly. Pray for me, for thy name means much to me Margaret. I can see Elizabeth is waiting for me at the end of the hall, such a light. Thou prayest well for me. I bid thee farewell with gratitude from my heart, evil though it was at one time. Remember Margaret well."

It puzzled me how she knew my name and to this day I still do not know. Confirming the existence of Margaret Pakenham was relatively easy. It took Wally no time at all to trace her from the information she had provided. Records concerning Gatcombe House date back to the Domesday Book of 1085 when it was owned by a man by the name of William Fitz Stur. The word Stur is believed to mean 'strong'. Sadly, however, the Stur family ran dry of males and the property passed by marriage into a new family, the Lisle's; but these too contracted the same problem. Again the daughter heir carried the estate into a new family, the Bremshotts, in the year 1446. By 1468 however the male line of Bremshott is snuffed out, leaving

Gatcombe in the hands of old man Bremshott's two daughters – Elizabeth and Margaret.

The sisters married, Elizabeth to John Dudley and Margaret to John Pakenham. Of the fate of these two and their families it is recorded that Elizabeth had a son, Edmund, the notorious lawyer who was put to death on the orders of big Henry VIII. Elizabeth died in 1499 and was spared the sight of her son's execution; but knavery must have been in the blood for grandson John, made Duke of Northumberland, it was who in a daring move some fifty years later attempted to promote his own interests by marrying his boy Guildford to Lady Jane Grey and declared her Queen of England. This did not best please Mary Tudor and she executed the lot of them. (Incidentally I found young Guildford Dudley and his beloved Lady Jane haunting the terrible Tower of London.)

Margaret Pakenham died in the year 1509, and she too left a son; but his own efforts to continue the line of Pakenham ended with two daughters and so again the house passed out of the family. Thus Margaret had been waiting for nearly 500 years lamenting the letter. Gatcombe House would have changed much during the long period of her haunting, but the ghost of Margaret Pakenham has now gone. She no longer haunts the house she regarded as her prison, and the beautiful park and lake; but she would have been present and watched during the next occupation of Gatcombe by a great family, the Worsleys. And they fared little better than their predecessors.

SPARKS FLY IN THE HOUSE OF LOVE

There is an old oil painting of a nobleman with fine ruff and cuffs and an amiable round-eyed face. The good knight Sir John Oglander stands hand on hip staring out of his picture, unravaged by the historic events yet to so affect his life; his fine goatee beard and exploding moustache seem ungreyed. Sir John lived during the years 1585 to 1665 and held the post of High Sheriff and Lieutenant of Portsmouth.

In his odd moments Sir John scribbled a famous notebook suggesting a few rules for husbandry, advice to his descendents, a favourite recipe or two and an analysis of the curious comings and goings of his neighbours. He recalls the first of the Worsleys to settle on the Island, Giles, whose attempts to produce a son and heir eventually resulted in the form of Thomas, a man of "unsettled brain", in fact quite "the maddest fellow that ever this Island bred". Even the good knight was at a loss to note all the pranks wrought by mad Tom Worsley.

His son Bowyer was one to upset the neighbours and this is no surprise, given the family's appetite for partymaking; his entry into Christian life was something of a memorable occasion according to Sir John. Worsley junior's Christening "was the greatest drinking and uncivil mirth that ever I knew," says he. "The Earl of Holderness was one of the Godfathers. After dinner they were to drink the healths and he had provided one hundred musketeers, fifty in the garden and fifty in the court, and at every health these must come in and discharge into the parlour, where they drank as much smoke as wine."* Before long the estate was half-wrested from mad Tom and sold off.

The next attempt to populate the Island with Worsleys took the form of James from Lancashire. While bad Edmund Dudley festered in the Tower of London awaiting his fate, young James won favour with King Henry. He made James Worsley Groom of the Royal Wardrobe, then Keeper of the Lions and other beasts in the Tower; then King Henry gave him the Island to mind. And many consider James Worsley a lucky man.

James chose to reside a few miles down the road from Gatcombe, in fair Appledurcombe House in its pretty valley near the sea. Henry visited the Island with his minister Cromwell, the mad "mauler of monks", and rewarded the family with some spoils from the monasteries; he even offered James' eldest son, Richard, Cromwell's post as Constable of Carisbrooke Castle when the mauler was beheaded.

The family busied themselves buying up country houses, one took a liking to Gatcombe and made it his own. Appledurcombe was to be the principal seat of the Worsleys and Gatcombe home of the second son. On becoming senior in the family, Richard Worsley assumed the rôle of Captain of the Island and spent his days building forts and tower defences against the threat of French invasion; and other times breaching the defences of his young dairymaid, Mary Targett. No doubt Richard Worsley watched in despair as did Henry when the flagship *Mary Rose* sank in the waters before the French invasion fleet. Though no doubt he took some

[*A Royalist's Notebook. The Commonplace Book of Sir John Oglander, Kt, of Nunwell. Trans. Francis Bamford. Constable & Co. 1936.]

revenge when chasing off the Frenchmen who attempted to ransack the Island in frustration at the King of England's reluctance to come out and do battle. Richard Worsley died in the year 1565. Perhaps the ghostly Mary Targett was there when two years later a terrible explosion blew up the gatehouse, killing his two "natural" sons.

*　　*　　*

Billingham Manor is said to be the most haunted house on the Island. Like Gatcombe, this manor was acquired by the Worsleys and brought into the family empire. Legend has it that the ghostly head of Charles I can be seen there sometimes, and no doubt this is due to the fame of the Worsleys' attempts to rescue the king from Carisbrooke Castle and get him away to safety. The plan was to hide him in Billingham's revolving bookcase and although Charles refused, the attempt only served to hasten his removal to London.

On a visit to the manor I did not find Charles' head but the ghost of a woman. It was in July 1978 when I was invited by the owners to help them. They were being disturbed at night by strange noises and, more alarmingly, the sound of a woman screaming. Guests of the owners also had heard the noises and some of them were very

Billingham Manor.

18

upset by it. Other people had reported smelling a strong perfume in the house.

Again I was accompanied by Wally and Jenny Gibbons. We all were welcomed by the gentleman of the manor who introduced his wife, a lady who looked as pale as any ghost. Perhaps she had experienced one fright too many for she seemed most ill at ease and fearful. The couple told us we could go into any room we wished and so in a group we began in the square entrance hall. In its centre stood a large walnut table with a bowl of faded mixed flowers. A few white rose petals had dropped onto the surface.

There was a perfume and I looked at the flowers, amazed there could be any fragrance left. I smelt them and shook my head. No, it was not rose but the smell of lillies. I thought it must be Jenny's or the lady's perfume, yet Jenny was sniffing the air like a hound to a scent and asked if I could smell anything. We all could, faint but unmistakable.

Even Wally was wrinkling his nose and I noticed him looking at the lady of the manor and she wore an expression of faint disgust. It made me laugh and Wally quickly turned and began pacing the room as if he could trace the direction from which the smell was coming. Wally was a scientist involved with fish oils and I often wondered, with all the smells he was subjected to, whether he ever could smell properly. He looked determined that day.

In the large drawing room the smell was stronger. The room was full of an assortment of faded furniture from various periods, a tattered embroidered shawl thrown over the back of a well-worn sofa. A door led into the library filled with dusty old books, and under the window a writing desk covered in papers.

From then on we were alone, the owners did not wish to come upstairs. Some people do not like to be present during the release and wait elsewhere. I imagine their concerned expressions and serious thoughts and wonder what must go through their minds. Calling the pest controllers for infestations is one thing, but ghost clearance is something that gives many people the spooks. Up the wide staircase to the first floor, the first bedroom was beautiful if a little faded in its glory, like the flowers. As I entered the room I immediately felt more agitated and anxious. The feeling had been building gradually and in this room it was strong. Very strong.

A big double bed dominated the room, its dark wood lightened by a bright shawl spread across its width. Nearby stood a large ottoman and various chairs and tables. In the facing wall were two large windows offering a pretty view over the lawn and flower-filled garden. Each window had a wide seat and I knew it was there I had to wait. I sat on one side while Jenny and Walter sat watching me from the other. The garden looked fresh and lush after a morning rain shower, peaceful and serene – not at all like I was feeling there inside that room. I found some paper and a pencil and waited. There was not a sound to be heard.

A terrible clanging of metal on metal filled the room and made me wince. Then a scream. Another scream, longer and more pained, then another. I managed to quickly scribble what the voice was crying . . .

". . . I entreat thee please, please do not kill him. I love him. Please Edward please! I plead with thee on my knees. Oh God! The blood. Release me from this, release me. Oh hear me. No-one listens. They only see. Release me I entreat thee!"

There was a pause and the voice sounded more steady.

". . . I married into the Worsley family with a feeling of trepidation. Edward was a man who possessed a rage I was terrified of. The night of terror I re-live in the room where I was found in the arms of my true love. I admit I deceived my husband yet the wild passionate wrath he showed was so frightening. A destructive force gave him the skill of handling the sword I had no knowledge he possessed. I begged and entreated him, assuaged him to give us his pity, his forgiveness. He listened not and I saw my true love killed by Edward Worsley, the man I was wed to.

My husband was in his cups when he attacked my true love, down the staircase into the garden with swords clashing. I threw a scent bottle at Edward that I picked up in haste, but alas missed him.

My lover had always behaved with unimpaired cordiality towards Edward. I indulged myself in an extravagance of grief and took to my bed after much swooning. Then Edward was feared for my wits although my contumacious behaviour he could not forgive. After I had been ensconced in my bedchamber a noise assaulted my ears due to a concourse of many people. I know not what they did or where they took the remains of my lover.

My wits were addled and kind words from friends meant nothing. The swords, that final thrust. Screams, mine or his?"

There was a sigh.

"Thank God for an ear to speak into. The sound has gone. There is silence now, a mist is descending. Throughout my time of reliving the past I have experienced a feeling of desolation and the guilt of causing my husband to kill a man through his frivolous and profligate wife. Now through the mist I see a light which gets larger and brighter. I hear voices. Can it be that now I am released from all earthly memories? Loneliness has left me and we are together in love, perfection, peace. The mist is clearing. I am released from bondage and am free ..."

I put down the pencil and sighed, releasing the breath I had been holding all the while. I am always anxious during this strange exchange that I might "lose" the ghost, interrupt the release and somehow put them in a worse state. I don't know why I worry like this, for I have never lost one yet. Anyhow I do not wish to start.

After she had finished speaking I felt a great peace within myself, the agitation and bad atmosphere had left the room. This is the sign the ghost has gone. They do not come back, whatever anyone may think. Any further haunting activity in the house will be due to another ghost – multiple hauntings are not uncommon.

The owners of the house have since told me they had no more trouble with sword fights, screams or perfume. All gone, I am pleased to say, and no doubt the ghost is too. Some ghosts, but by no means all, are somehow trapped, reliving the traumatic incident over and over. Now she is at peace and so too is the bedroom.

In his study of *The Manor Houses of the Isle of Wight*, Ron Winter identifies this to be the ghost of Jane Leigh who married Edward Worsley in the year 1708. She died in 1741 having been kept a virtual prisoner in the house afterwards and was buried in the church graveyard of Gatcombe where Edward was laid to rest.*

There were other ghosts at Billingham Manor, of Francis I will tell you later; but also haunting there was Sarah. We found her in the garden and when she spoke her voice was small and scared:

"'Twas in the stables I met him every night. Billy we calls him. He be a strong man, I be that proud of walking out with Billy; then he got the old man's temper up and had to leave. I be that sad as I be having his child."

[*The Manor Houses of The Isle of Wight*. C. W. R. Winter. Dovecote Press 1984.]

21

There was a sniffle. Then:

"Billy came to see me just once and then had to go away. The old man had an awful temper and him being a Preacher he always said that one had to be honest and virtuous, industrious and pure. I knew he would be cross with me when he heard about the child. I didn't know what to do and kept me corsets tightly laced so no-one would see."

Sarah's voice became calm, almost confiding.

"One day I swooned when I was washing the back kitchen. 'Perhaps she is too tightly laced,' the cook said. So they loosened me stays so find out I be having a baby. The old man was cross and quite religious with giving me a whole sermon to meself. The mistress was kinder and came to the attic where I slept, to talk to me. Said she would see I was alright. Everyone wanted to know the father, but I wouldn't tell. Preacher wouldn't speak much, except to read me passages from the Bible. 'Whore of Babylon,' he called me once. That upset me, I ain't no whore. I love Billy."

Sarah paused, and the moment gave me a chance to turn the paper and be ready. She wanted to tell her tale.

"When I was weak from having the baby the mistress said not to work 'till afterwards, and let me stay in the attic. She gave me some stitching to do, making a gown for the baby. She was kind, the mistress, not like he be. Wished I could have told Billy he was going to be a father, but didn't know where he be. Found out afterwards he had gone to sea and got himself drownded. Then the pains started. I tried not to scream as the mistress had some friends staying with her. Cook and the other maids were kind and helped me.

They took me baby away, said I musn't see him as he was born dead. I cried a lot then. Young 'elen who just got took on came into the attic and gave me a tiny box, inside was some dark hair. Said before they took the little boy away she cut off some hair as it were dark and quite a lot like Billy's. So when I was up and doing again I hid the box with the hair safe behind the secret panel I found when polishing."

Sarah's voice began to tremble, as if panic was setting in again.

"Now I have looked for my child, I can't find him and forgotten the panel. Everything being changed! I have to stay 'til

22

I find my baby or his hair. Billy has gone on now I know, but I must stay. I go all round the house looking. Can't remember. Everything gone!"

There was a long pause.

"I am happy someone knows now, as I wasn't a whore of Babylon like the Preacher said, I really wasn't. I loved my Billy and we would have wed. Where did they put my baby, where is his hair? I just wants something to have of my own. Must keep looking. Everything different. No-one can help me, though they may know now I wasn't a bad girl. Sarah."

It is next to impossible to identify exactly who little Sarah was or where she came from; and it may be that she still roams Billingham Manor in search of her child. It is possible to identify who her employer, the Preacher and owner of the manor, might have been – the Reverend James Worsley lived there at the end of the 1700s. He was also vicar of Saint Olave's church in the village of Gatcombe.

* * *

Appledurcombe House in Wroxall was the grandest of the Worsley residences. It sits in the pretty rippling valley sheltered by downs and cradled in a natural amphitheatre of earth. The present building dates back to the time of Robert Worsley, for he it was who demolished the old Tudor house and rebuilt to his own taste a square Corinthian building with low projecting pavilions; with triumphal arches for chimneys, and doors and windows decorated with mouldings, scrolls and drapery. He even added the mask of a satyr above the east door.

Appledurcombe House.

23

Robert spent many happy years on his pet project until the money ran out and tragedy struck, as his two sons died during his lifetime. He could not complete the work on the park and when he died the house passed again to cousins of the family and finally into the care of Sir Richard in the year 1768. From royal favourites of kings and queens, the Worsleys were a powerful and wealthy family with many important connections; the heirs and daughters married into the very best of families. There were Knights and Captains and Constables and even would-be royal rescuers; they were Members of Parliament and military officers. The Worsley family had known some glory and when Sir Richard, seventh baronet Worsley of Appledurcombe, pleased his government by ensuring Parliamentary elections for his local borough went in their favour, he was rewarded with an important appointment in the Court of King George III; and in a happy moment George saw fit to make him Governor of the Isle of Wight. With the proposed marriage to the very lovely and very wealthy Miss Seymour Fleming, no doubt Sir Richard Worsley expected to continue the family's success on into the next century. In 1775 they were married. Seven years later they were divorced.

Sir Richard's divorce action against his wife cited neighbour George Bisset in the proceedings. Lady Worsley, complained Sir Richard, had eloped with Bisset and the scandal had become nothing less than public entertainment. He sued the pair for damages, demanding £20,000, and when his wife gave testimony in the High Court she was accused by the prosecution of having thirty-five lovers. Lady Worsley was forced to admit that George Bisset was indeed the latest in a long list of lovers, twenty-seven of whom she could remember. The judge in the case maintained a serious expression when he awarded Sir Richard one shilling in compensation for his trouble.

Sadly, the publicity forced Sir Richard to resign from both Court and the Governorship of the Island. He decided to leave the country for a while. For five years he roamed the Classical lands of the Mediterranean, adventuring and collecting paintings and statues and gems, and even a fair selection of ancient Greek marbles from broken temples. His treasures were brought back to the Island, and Appledurcombe House became a museum. From inside the house he banished the fine painting by Reynolds of his wife, preferring instead a huge canvas of Daniel in the Lion's Den.

Sir Richard decided to complete the work on the house and park as a fitting setting to his treasures. He removed the formal ordered gardens and in their place created a nice carefully designed and crafted natural look. For good measure he built obelisks and mock castles to please the eye and remember the family's past glory. On the crest of a hill at the northern entrance there rose the great Freemantle Gate, a triumphal stone arch and wrought iron gateway to commemorate the nobility of the estate of Worsley.

It was one year after our visit to Billingham Manor that we found the ghost of Lady Worsley. She was haunting the Freemantle Gate. Nearby stand the ruins of an old cottage, presumably once the gate-house. I had felt drawn there and we made ourselves comfortable beside the gateposts and waited in the warm sunshine of a summer's afternoon. The gate is no longer used for traffic, yet the track remains with deep grooves in the earth where once carriages transported their elegant passengers through the woodland on either side.

The three of us waited, I more anxious than the other two, who were sitting quietly, listening to the light breeze through the leaves. Then in a voice both confident and yet confiding, Lady Seymour Worsley told me of the sweetest bed of all.

Freemantle Gate, Appledurcombe.

25

Lady Worsley.

" . . . I declare he was the most handsome man I had seen. Dark hair, brown skin, twinkling blue eyes and so tall. I had returned from Paris and London to find this Adonis open the gate for my carriage. As he touched his forelock I granted him a smile and a nod. Such a stranger must be investigated by one who took lovers like changing a gown.

The next day I made it my business to find out who he was and now I am here looking for the rough peasant who meant more to me than my husband or the ton that I picked my lovers from. This Adonis was staying with his parents who were the gatekeepers. He had his wife with him and a mewling babe, she wet nursing an infant of a member of the household. We met when I let the pink curling feather from my hat loose to float to his feet. This started a conversation. He was tongue-tied at first, poor handsome creature, but to be tumbled in the hay like a village maid was a new experience. Now where is he?

I left to return to London but thought of him in my dreams. To Vauxhall, to the Assembly Rooms, to the arms of yet another lover, to balls and routs. Then to return to find him still here waiting. Oh his hands so rough yet his caresses so soft and gentle as no other man. He was sent away when his wife had finished her duties as a wet nurse. La, how that woman irked me.

Jealousy was my middle name methinks, but never again did I inhale the pungent scent of the ferns without recalling the sweetest bed of all. My husband cared not. The most famous of all the Worsleys. A rake. A serpent, but he did improve the house, that much I give credit for. Now here I am waiting for what I do not know. The greatest of lovers is not here. The cottage so different, ruined, all ruined. No roadway, people in ugly clothes, women dressed as men. What can I do? Pray tell me. La, but you all wear such strange attire.

One in pantaloons that are straight and one in a long skirt

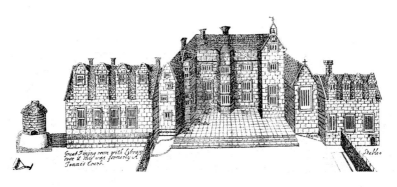

A contemporary engraving of old Appledurcombe House.

without several petticoats. One in a skirt so short. Fie I feel faint at the thought; yet I know these strangers from another century have freed me from ever seeking my Adonis, the man whose body I yearned for. My sin was not just adultery, yet over and over again and out of my station in life. I see a shaft of light, a green band and I can go onwards." I heard her sigh.

"I pray do not abuse my soul where I am to go. Treat me kindly, repentance will be sweet, I am so certain. Goodbye forever gateway and cottage. Farewell."

I heard a crack and Walter was stretching his legs, adjusting his pantaloons and I laughed out loud. I suppose the skirt I was wearing just above the knees would be considered short in her day. It surprised me that a woman who took so many lovers could be shocked over clothing.

Sir Richard eventually abandoned Appledurcombe and spent his final years in a cottage by the sea while the museum gathered dust. At the time of his death in 1805 the pictures were left in piles on the floor. Lady Seymour Worsley never did marry George Bisset and some have since wondered why.

* * *

In the year 1805 Appledurcombe House became the home of Lady Henrietta, niece of Sir Richard. She married and her husband Yarborough, from off the Island, thought it a good base for his yachting visits. He rearranged the library then decided to sell the lot, for it was not to his taste. The treasures were removed.

In 1867 the Reverend Pound turned the house into a college for young gentlemen and failed. In 1901 it was the temporary home for an order of Benedictine monks, then for troops stationed in the wars. Queen Mary took a fancy to fair Appledurcombe but in 1943 a land mine fell nearby and blew out the roof and windows. Any attempts at restoration were considered "idealistic" and by 1950 someone suggested it had "disintegrated beautifully in all the morbid shades of a fading bruise".*

What was left is now maintained by a public body. They have done a good job too. This is fortunate for at Appledurcombe a ghost remains and will not leave. Her name is Henrietta and I have seen her on several occasions. Not only has she appeared to me but also to my friend Sue Robertson. We have visited this ruin together and have seen her quite clearly.

I am not the only person in the world to experience what might be called 'flashbacks' – brief glimpses of the past being enacted before our eyes – or timeslips as I prefer to call them. As amazing as it may sound it is not an uncommon phenomenon, in fact such experiences are possibly more widespread than the ability to see ghosts.

Both Sue and myself experience such visions and when we do neither of us say anything until it has finished and then we compare what happened. It is always identical. During visits to Appledurcombe we have watched as rooms momentarily transform from a dripping stone shell to a lavishly furnished drawing room. There are blue velvet curtains at the windows and a richly coloured carpet on the floor. On one occasion Lady Henrietta could be seen playing a spinet. She appears each time wearing a different gown, so she obviously has access to a full wardrobe.

She does not often speak but one day she informed me she had no intention of leaving as she is so happy there with her lover, who presumably also is a ghost. Quite how this arrangement has come about I have no idea. One day I went there alone and saw Lady Henrietta come down a staircase and enter the library. In reality this room is a shell with nothing in it. I watched as she passed across to a large bookcase. I could see many bookcases, a table and chairs and she came towards me smiling. In her hands she carried a book, Chaucer's *Canterbury Tales*. She opened it at *The Miller's Tale* but as I extended my hand to take it, she and the book vanished, and I was left standing in the ruins of a once beautiful room. Each year Sue and I return and visit Lady Henrietta as we feel this is what she wants, for we have come to regard her as a friend.

[*Appledurcombe House*. L. O. J. Boynton. English Heritage (quoting Rose Macaulay, *Pleasure of Ruins*). London 1953.]

CHAPTER THREE

THE LAST POSTS AT THE HOUSE OF BISSET

F
OR REASONS best known to himself, George Bisset destroyed his magnificent home of Knighton Gorges rather than let his daughter and her clergyman husband inherit the estate. Old George moved into his gardener's cottage and watched as his fine Elizabethan manor overlooking the pretty vale of Newchurch was pulled down brick by brick.

Some say tragedy and curse enshroud the house, for in times past its owner was one of the men who visited Thomas Becket at Canterbury cathedral and took part in hacking off the top of the Archbishop's head. In the long history of the house of Knighton Gorges tragedy has indeed visited; though chances are many strange things would inevitably take place during the passage of time. But old George's behaviour was certainly peculiar.

All that remains of the once great manor house is a pair of gateposts. There have been many reports of unearthly incidents,

The remaining gateposts at Knighton Gorges.

some claim to have heard the sound of laughter and music, of ghostly party-making drifting up the valley. There have been two reported accounts when witnesses have actually seen the house. There is also a report from fifty years ago of a young man who visited the Island for a walking holiday. During his journey nearby he knocked on the door of a cottage and asked for lodging. That night as he sat for supper he asked who lived in the house along the track, the big Elizabethan-looking place. He said he had passed by the gateposts and was nearly killed by a carriage and horses thundering through the gateway and making for the house at full gallop.

The young man had picked himself out of the ditch and followed the carriage up to the house to confront the reckless driver. From inside he heard music and laughter and although he hammered on the door, no-one answered. He found a window and peered through a gap in the curtains and saw a party in full fling, fancy Georgian dress; he tapped on the window but still no-one noticed. Finally he decided to leave and find somewhere nearby to stay the night. The wife of the cottage owner asked where the house was, and the young man took out his map and pointed to the place he had seen. No house was there. For no house exists on that site. The ghostly carriage has often been seen. But only once has it stopped.

"The carriage was late arriving," spoke the ghost of the gateposts. "I was invited as a guest, met him in London. Wonderful island, not like at sea or in London. Now everything gone. Pigot my name, reached the rank of Admiral. My fault telling the man to make haste, I had spent too long with some fine port. It was as we approached the gates a figure was afore us; could not blame the man as I told him not to spare the horses. To arrive as a guest on a lovely island and being responsible for the idiot's death. Methinks it was only I to blame."

The Admiral's voice sounded loud beside me and I could hear the sound of harness from the carriage.

"The son of a servant with no wits in the head that was crushed. A small amount of gold coins and the matter was closed. I enjoyed my visit and would not let the idiot's death spoil this respite from duties. I told no-one and my host said the least said the better, even my wife and family were not enlightened.

I did not return to the house, yet so oft heard in my dreams the horses' hooves and the scream of the lumbering idiot.

Therefore I was drawn to the spot when I made the longest voyage all must make at the end of their lives.

I am sad I was not bold enough to see the idiot had a Christian burial. To be bundled into the ground like a dog, his widowed mother silenced with gold, the horses' hooves smashing his skull . . ."

There was a long pause.

"Now I have confessed I hope and pray I shall go towards the brilliance I see, yet reach it I have been unable. If the horses stop I know I can go onwards and the years will not have been wasted. Please accept my gratitude for finding me, curious folk have looked yet have never listened with their inner ear, which is rare. Thank you."

The ghostly admiral also spoke a phrase in Latin which when translated read: "Oh, if Jupiter would restore to me the past years."

Again Wally had a name to work on and having contacted the Naval College at Greenwich managed to confirm the identity of Hugh Pigot, R.N., Admiral and Commander-in-Chief, West Indies. It

Knighton Gorges.

was in the year 1769 he was in charge of the Portsmouth Division of the Marines and doubtless found himself with an invitation to a party at Knighton Gorges. In the year 1782 Admiral Pigot sailed for the West Indies on board *HMS Jupiter*. I can only guess he was lamenting his fate to the God Jupiter and not his ship.

CHAPTER FOUR

OF GAMES AND PATIENCE

I WAS CALLED back to Billingham Manor: again the release of one ghost had, it seemed, raised the hopes of another. Jane Worsley had gone together with the clash of swords and wafts of perfume, but another ghost was making its presence felt more than usual. Again it was not the ghostly head of Charles I, but a complete 'body' in the form of Francis.

My encounter with Francis Worsley was one of the most extraordinary of all my experiences, for he actually managed to move me – not just with his undoubted charm, but physically. Although Francis never confirmed this, it is believed he was the son of the Reverend James Worsley, Rector of Gatcombe church. Rev. Worsley managed to produce a son two years before his death and the boy's name was Francis, born in the year 1796. Francis, I must admit, was one of my favourite ghosts of all time.

I remembered the tree-lined drive to the manor house and the warm greeting of the owner who welcomed us once again. As we passed through the hall I noticed the flowers on the table were much fresher and I could detect a scent from them. Altogether the house felt somewhat brighter – perhaps it was the burst of sunshine through the window flooding the hallway.

Once again we were offered the run of the house and began our search in the library. The owner was showing us his collection of books; he seemed much more at ease this time, perhaps he had realised this removal of ghosts was not the macabre séance-type activity of movie myth.

It was the same 'team' as before – Walter and Jenny and me. We were all admiring the books and talking when a most puzzling thing occurred. I was no longer with the others, but without any effort on my part I found myself sitting in a window seat upstairs, in one of the main bedrooms in another wing of the manor. I had no time to wonder how I had gotten there as immediately a man's voice came from the centre of the room, although I could see no-one.

"I have been condemned to remain here. My folly and sins outweighed my virtues. I am resigned yet show myself to a few. One who listens is a reward for my patience. My soul may become free as this chain could be broken.

In this house I cheated. I played faro and other such games. I had a looking glass or pier glass which reflected others' hands. I held a fifth ace among the ruffles of my sleeve and because of this I won much. I caused a man to shoot himself, so I remain here. Yet now an ear to listen, to confess to. What joy will await me! My felicitations to you. I am your servant ma'am . . ."

As I finished writing, the door of the bedroom creaked and opened slowly. I held my breath and then I saw Jenny's head appear. "Oh there you are," she sighed, "you vanished and we've been searching everywhere. One minute you were by my side, the next . . . gone."

I followed Jenny downstairs and there was much excited talk and questioning. The lady of the manor provided tea and I was pleased to see there was more colour in her cheeks and a happier bearing.

I was told it was impossible to move about the house silently as almost every floorboard creaked; only the ghosts could do it. How I had managed it the others were at a complete loss to explain or understand. After the questions I decided to return to the bedroom to see if I could get any more, and as I climbed the stairs I smiled as Jenny and Walter and the couple of the house were tip-toeing up the stairs behind me. I shut the door as I entered; and Francis spoke again in his lovely soft romantic voice.

"May I present myself again ma'am and solicit your kindness for listening to me. I find you have an agreeable nature and wish I had met one such as you in my life which I fear I did not make the most of. No doubt you were around at that time and such a misfortune upon us not meeting has now been corrected. I feel I may have behaved in an impetuous manner to pull you to a quiet room away from the eyes and ears of others.

I am hoping you will visit my lovely manor again and without any flummery I shall materialise for you alone. I shall once again show the room. This may not necessarily be the same one. Oh the foolishness of men to believe that one stays in just one room. I roam all over the manor yet cannot show you my handsome self today. Forgive me if I sound a vain man.

I shall look forward to our meeting which will be our last as I shall go on after that towards the light, as only then will the chain that keeps me bound to the manor be broken. Your servant ma'am."

It puzzled me why Francis could not leave immediately. Did he have things to attend to before he went for good? I tried to explain as best I could to the couple what had happened and that it was necessary to return another time to complete the work. I tried to reassure them it would not be long and not to worry, though I had no idea quite what Francis was up to.

On the way back to the manor the following week Jenny jokingly said she would pin her skirt to mine so I couldn't vanish without taking her with me. In the end she did not go so far but it made me laugh to see how closely she kept to my side as soon as we arrived. We stood talking to the lady of the house and were invited into the dining room. Then suddenly I was with them no longer, but sitting on the floor in the middle of an attic room with steep sloping ceilings. Around me were chests, trunks and an old rocking horse. I gazed about me in amazement, as I had no idea how I had reached the attic. Then the pleasant voice seemed to come from one corner of the attic.

"Greeting ma'am from this erring creature whose footsteps have been heard and whose figure has been seen. I have so oft repented for the sins which need not have been committed, gambling, cheating and lying over and over again. Now having spoken in a voice which has echoed in the ear of another I find I can proceed further into a higher place and the strange unknown way this has happened leaves me with a feeling of awe.

My thanks. I had always favoured dark-haired ladies. My name for the record can be Francis, but this is of no consequence. I bid thee farewell and shall always be, in spirit, your servant ma'am."

As I finished writing I looked up and saw him so clearly. His face and feet had a misty quality to them but his coat was clear enough and very lovely, made of some rich dark red material with gold embroidery down the front and on the wide cuff and pockets. I could see frothy lace at his cuffs and neck, his knee breeches were white and so were his stockings. On his head he wore a grey wig tied at the back with a black bow.

I am no artist but quickly did my best to sketch him as he turned and faced me and then made a deep, extravagantly flowing bow. I watched with delight as he walked proudly across the room and disappeared in front of the wall. I did not feel in the least bit frightened, just excited, realising how wonderful it is to be granted the gift

Francis at Billingham Manor on 27/7/78.
In the attic.

Sketch of Francis in the attic at Billingham Manor, 27th July 1978.

of sight to experience this charming rogue so clearly. And Francis was in awe of it all!

I became aware of banging and voices calling me. I slowly climbed down the steep flight of stairs to a door which opened onto a landing. There I found the others and the two men had been struggling to open the door which they swore had been locked tight. They had become alarmed as Jenny pointed out I was there beside her and then I wasn't. For me the explanations simply would not come, and to this day I do not know how I came to travel up not one but two flights of creaky stairs without being seen or heard.

Such a thing has never happened since and there have been all sorts of strange experiences. I must add, looking back, this was one of my most pleasant encounters with a ghost; and I do have dark hair.

As for Billingham Manor, some have claimed to have seen King Charles' ghostly head. But this seems improbable to me. Perhaps it was one of Francis' pranks. I suspect so. Some ghosts are stronger than others, as with living human beings, and Francis certainly had the power to roam the entire house and could even transport objects – me for example.

No doubt during his long imprisonment he has amused himself with the residents and, together with Lady Jane's screams and perfume throwing and sword fighting, the house has been a difficult place in which to dwell. Others have stayed there and sensed nothing to disturb their peace of mind. Some however could not remain. The ghosts of Billingham Manor have terrified plenty of those who have passed through its doors – some quicker than others. Families and servants, wedding guests and even an Army General from overseas grew weary of the unearthly interruptions in his wartime billet.

As I think back to Lady Jane in the bedroom I do sometimes wonder over the scenes of startled guests; and then Francis chuckling in the doorway holding up a turnip with a wig.

The lady owner of Billingham sold the house soon after and moved away. It is said that on the day of her departure someone had set about her packed suitcase which lay on her former bed and sent its contents flying round the room.

But Francis had gone.

Perhaps it was the ghostly Sarah searching for her child . . .

CHAPTER FIVE

GHOSTS OF THE WILD

H AUNTINGS AREN'T always in creepy old houses and mansions. They are just as common in quiet country lanes, fields and woodlands. Indeed, there are just as many ghosts out-of-doors as inside, and people are generally less aware of these. Woods and forests can often have an eerie feeling about them; some might think it is simply something to do with the shape of old twisting trees in the dusk light, or the sound of rustling in the undergrowth.

Many people do have a sense of apprehension about such places and I must admit I have found plenty of ghosts in the wild. It is not that ghosts are especially attracted to forests; they attract living people, and living people do things which keep them earthbound. Ghosts haunt the sites that had a special relevance for them when alive – and so often it is a forest.

To find a ghost in a country setting is different. Any old building is likely to have a ghost or two, but outside I am helped. I am not a Spiritualist and have never thought of myself in that way; but like everyone else I have what you might call 'guardian angels', or guides. Everybody has them, and they are usually close friends or relatives from other times who have asked or been asked to help a living soul through their lifetime. Chances are a painter has a painter as a guide, and a mechanic a mechanic. It's the way it is.

In the same way that I have not always been able to hear ghosts, I have not always been able to hear these guides who are responsible for me; but in recent years – roughly as long as I've been hearing ghosts – I have come to know them well. It is they who find ghosts who need help in lonely locations and tell me where I must go to release them.

Ghosts in houses and other buildings can generally be confirmed because there is usually a documented history which can give clues, if not complete identification; but those ghosts in country locations can rarely be identified for certain. They are usually ordinary individuals who like most of us leave little trace in historical documentation. However, if proof of their existence is required it can sometimes be found in the possessions they leave behind – and from time to time these are unearthed.

I never work alone – always I am accompanied by one or more people. Usually there is nothing to fear from those spirits we set out to help, but often there are difficulties as care is needed in the surroundings they lead us to, sometimes through mud and earth-slides, or making us crawl through brambles or barbed wire; even sometimes a dangerous scramble up or down cliffs. On such expeditions all that is needed is courage, determination, and some helpers armed with trowels ready to dig and witness.

It rarely takes a long time for the ghost to speak. Most are desperate for release and often I have to tell them to slow down or wait while I find another piece of paper. Most really are in a hurry to get away, having waited for so long. By all accounts it is not much fun being a ghost.

I had been told there was someone who needed help in Borthwood Copse, and this time Wally and I were joined by a lady named Doreen; she had a car and would often provide us with transport to release a ghost. Although we took our missions very seriously, with Doreen there was always plenty of laughter, for when we were together we could see the fun in everything. She also had a way with Wally; she would tease him a little, as he could be most serious.

Borthwood Copse.

However, that particular afternoon we all were serious as we walked deeper into the woods. The large trees shut out much of the sunlight and a feeling of eeriness crept over us all and we fell into silence. The path we followed narrowed and on either side the ground was covered with ivy and trailing brambles. I sensed we were to leave the path and go to the left which meant finding our way through that undergrowth. We walked carefully and slowly towards a big old gnarled tree and there I came to a halt, for a voice spoke and I nearly jumped out of my skin at first.

"... Good morrow sweet mistress ... Thou stands near where I was struck down at eventide in the twenty-second year of my life. Ah how I would like to cull garlands to bind the brow of my beloved, or write sweet verse to see how her rosebud lips would bestow a kiss. Yet to taste the delights that were promised when wedded bliss would be mine was denied me by a villain. A foreigner by looks, yet only a glimpse I had of him.

A ship would have brought him from a distant land. He carried a strange sling and the shot of a coin from that dastardly sling caught me on my forehead. I should have travelled on to paradise but somehow I was held back. I lay on the ground for nigh on a sennight before being given a Christian burial. I was named Edward after many kings. The coin that took my life lays near thee. Spread around in a circle like the garlands I spoke about and take my love as gracefully as I give it."

How lovely sounded the old-fashioned flowery way of speech to Doreen and I. We stumbled through the tangled mass beneath our feet trying to find the coin. "Another Edward," I heard Wally mutter as he kicked around in the ivy. "We'll never find it, you know." Doreen and I giggled and he began to dig beside a clump of campions in flower. Doreen was turning over the earth near a rotting log and I clawed at the ivy between them.

You might think it an impossible feat to find something as small as a coin in a forest, especially as it may have been there for a hundred years or more. Falling leaves and boughs, growing plants and moving earth would hide it even more. I believe it would be impossible if it weren't for the help we receive from the ghost.

Sometimes they pull me to the spot where the object lies buried; other times I can see a 'spotlight' marking the ground – a circle of silver light – and this indicates where we must look. Not everyone sees the light. Not everyone sees the ghost.

At long last we were led to a place not far from where Wally had been digging. We gathered around the spot and dug deeper and there in the earth, like a sixpence in a Christmas pudding, lay the coin. Wally rolled it over in his hands and suggested it was a George I Hibernian coin. A penny, he said. It was an unpleasant experience to hold it in my hand, knowing it had caused a man's death, and I passed it back to Wally for safe keeping. I returned to the tree as I guessed the ghost had not gone.

"... To awake one morn by the song of the blackbirds and the May trees lifting their blossoms to greet the sun. To feel the love of a sweet maid within my grasp, then to be struck down and left like a dog. Ah how terrible is sorrow to a man. But now I have made contact and an opening appears before me.

The man followed me to steal my purse which was but a poor one. I too had many sins to bear as I was not always a pretty fellow with the maids. My thanks sweet mistress for thy attention. The light that shines forth is true love."

What a charming rogue he must have been. I was happy to be able to release him from haunting that unfriendly place. After cleaning the coin at home I discovered the date to be 1723 and from time to time since I look and remember the sweet-tongued charmer.

*   *   *

There is a saying "thieves stick together" and the next case is an extraordinary one in which three men happened to meet after death and found themselves haunting together. It was a surprise to learn that more than one ghost could be released at a time, if they are connected in some way. Bill and Ted and their new found friend John were not having such an excellent time where we found them – in the woods between Knighton and the Arreton Downs road.

The voice was deep and gruff:

"Cannot get towards the light. I am here with two other men. I never met them when I was alive. When I died I started along a narrow pathway towards a silver light and two other men joined me. We all realised we had something in common. We terrorized old people. We stole from them or burgled their houses and we often crept in while they slept. Yet we never met one another.

I am the one who appears to have brought the others as we floated in darkness. I remembered this spot where I threw away a piece I thought was worthless from an old man's house in

41

Brading. We are all here begging help and forgiveness. The world is wicked, but it is worse floating in the dark. My name is Ted and the others are Bill and John. Help us and see if the object can be discovered, somewhere higher where it got lodged."

Behind us was a small steep rise with very uneven ground below. We carefully picked our way through the brambles, stinging nettles and thistles all around. Wally was searching in an area of broken earth, but I had the feeling what we were looking for was higher up the rise. It was a mass of brambles and looked a painful scramble to get up so I carried on searching with Wally, but a few feet higher than the spot where I had heard Ted speak.

Suddenly I felt as if I was being lifted, and the next thing I found myself wedged between a small tree and a bramble bush three-quarters of the way up the slope. Walter was puzzled at how I managed to get so high so quickly but I reassured him I was okay and suggested I was there for a reason.

I had no idea how I got up there. I looked around and saw the earth by the bramble bush was soft, so carefully dug down with my trowel and soon found something and pulled it out. It was a piece of china. I clutched the object to my chest, scared to look for fear I would drop it or fall. Somehow a very scratched and dirty me returned to the base of the slope, not quite sure whether I had descended by my own efforts.

I held the thing in my hands, a tiny ornamental jug, vaguely shaped like a decapitated duck, with an emblem on the side – a souvenir from Paignton, Devon. As I examined it I half wondered whether I might be guilty of receiving stolen goods and asked Wally about this. Before he could answer I heard the sound of men's laughter, and then Ted's rough voice again.

"As there were three of us and we are strong physically, even if we are weak spiritually, we were able to pull you up the slope, ease you sideways and fix brambles onto you to hold you in position to find the ornament. Thank you for being so helpful. We were all sinful and did not respect our elders. Woe to those who do not.

We all died within a week of each other and that made it possible for us to link up. Thieves often stick together, they say, and it is true. Anyway, the path opens up and we shall all proceed onwards. Thanks to you."

And again I heard the sound of men's laughter, this time fading away as I showed Wally the ornamental jug and asked whether I would be implicated in their crime because I found it. If I could return it I would, but I guess the owner is long dead by now.

*   *   *

I could not help but smile when I read the confession of Charles and dug the horrible-looking creature out of the mud. We found the ghost of Charles haunting the cliffs at Gurnard. It had been raining heavily the night before and a cool wind was blowing that day; conditions were far from pleasant but I had a free afternoon and did not want to waste it. The clifftop path was very slippery with mud and by the time we reached the place where I knew the haunting was, the mud covered my shoes. I put a sheet of plastic on the ground so I could sit and write down anything I heard. Indeed I don't think conditions have ever been so bad for doing such work.

To make matters worse I dropped my pencil into a puddle, and so not only was the pencil muddy but also my hands and the paper I was to write on. Wally looked just as miserable and nearly as muddy as me when at last the ghost spoke. Or rather, growled.

"I was rotten through and through, just like a rotten apple. I appreciated nature though and when I saw a rare species of bird or butterfly I got quite excited. I was a great admirer of Darwin and went along with all his theories. I was bad and committed just about every sin except murder. I hated my fellow human beings, but as I said, I admired Darwin. He was the only person I would never have harmed.

I made a study of insect life and the more I studied the more I liked the uglier creatures. When I was given by a learned professor a present of an insect that had, so he informed me, belonged to Charles Darwin I treasured it. I used to sit on these cliffs by the hour studying these fascinating creatures. When I found I had lost my treasure it worried me very much. I cannot swear it really belonged to Darwin, I only had the professor's word for it.

I died a natural death, realising how many sins which I will not bore you with, I had committed. I was then back here seeking my insect. Find it please. I see it is very near you. My name is Charles too."

We started our search by slithering through the mud. There were some thick bramble bushes nearby and yet I felt drawn towards them and began digging. Then I noticed the silver light deeper into the bushes and I called Wally over. As the mud flew we saw something. I thought it was real and shuddered. We both just stood and stared at it for a while, neither of us wanting to touch it. "You pick it up," suggested Wally. So I had to. With some reluctance I pulled it from the ground and wiped away the mud. It was a metal locust about two and a half inches in length, absolutely perfect in every detail. No wonder we thought it real. The pair of us were in a very wet and muddy state, but I felt I had to return to the sheet of plastic I had been sitting on. I knew Charles wanted to speak some more. I did not have to wait long.

"I am pleased the insect has been found. I have roamed around here thinking of my many sins and at the same time I have been mentally gaining knowledge. Some of Darwin's theories are correct. I thought him a good man. Every insect is beautiful, however ugly it may appear to the human eye."

I heard a brief laugh.

"You flinched when you first saw it, that was natural. You will realise how beautiful it is in the eyes of the creator. Thank you for hearing me. I now go on to a silver circle of light that lifts me beyond the plane of Earth."

I was glad I was able to release this spirit, but more pleased the task was over. The locust has been admired by many people I have shown it to; but some refuse to hold it as it looks so realistic. I certainly shan't forget what I felt when first I saw it sticking out of the mud.

Wally and I spent most fine days releasing ghosts, accompanied by those who wished to come along and help. All of us were astounded at just how many poor souls there were in need of rescue and release.

"You can hear me, can't you?"asked the voice of a woman as we waited on the cliffs near Atherfield beach.

"I am so pleased. My name is Rachel. As a child I was very cruel. I would pull the legs off spiders. Many children do this but they soon get bored and grow out of it."

The wind was strong that day and it was difficult to find shelter so we sat huddled behind a bush. Nevertheless I could hear Rachel's voice quite clearly. She had a strong voice, piercing. She continued talking while I listened and wrote.

"I worked at a research establishment that experimented with animals. Mice, rats and monkeys. I had no compassion for any living creature. I hated worms and snakes as I lived in the country. I often saw grass snakes, sloe worms and even adders. I would chop them into bits. I enjoyed doing this. I know it is wrong, that is why I am trapped. A very dear friend gave me a bracelet like a snake. At first I liked it, then I grew to hate it. When we came to the Island for a few days I was walking along here, above where you are.

I saw a snake and killed it. I then did a strange thing. I threw the bracelet over the cliff edge. As the ground has slipped it fell down with loose stones. If you dig in them you could find it if you want to. This did cause a bitter quarrel and I found myself friendless. Why I wondered? No-one liked me. I know why now. Having told my story I shall proceed towards the brilliant light I see ahead. Thanks for listening. I hope you can find it. Perhaps you will wear it sometimes and think of me."

Amongst the stones at the foot of the cliff we retrieved the bracelet; it was a silver metal, intricately carved with flower-like swirls and scales. It had no clasp, only a spring which kept the thing together in the form of two snakes happily rubbing cheek to cheek.

THE WORLD'S MOST PATHETIC HAUNTING?

In the woods of Luccombe Chine there stands the remains of a house and its walled garden. The house has subsided and crumbled but some sections of the garden wall remain and the grey masonry can just be seen between the veil of ivy and bramble which now smothers it. There are stone steps leading up to nowhere and a few bricks and old slates litter the ground.

The ruins stand a long way off the path and the ground so uneven and dangerously sloped that few would dare climb around it. One afternoon Wally and I had decided to take a long walk in the area when I felt drawn off the path and stumbled through the brambles; I did not know where I was going and Wally followed, somewhat puzzled. It surprised us both to find the ruins as we had not known there was a house there and I guessed few other people do.

I felt great excitement around me, terrific excitement, and a voice was babbling to me even before I had paper and pencil; I told him to wait please as we made ourselves comfortable. It was fortunate I had plenty of paper as by the time I had jotted down all Percival had to say, my hand ached from overwork.

"As the son of a doctor I was expected to be the possessor of brains, wit, charm and personality. Instead I was stolid, tactless and clumsy. I lived in a fashionable suburb of London in the 1890s and endured the ridiculous name of Percival, and so often in my schooldays had to answer to 'Purse,' 'Moneybags' or even worse 'Val' which became 'Valley'.

I was not happy at school and I detested any form of sport. We were encouraged to learn cricket, but to me the ball that came so swiftly towards one was terrifying. At a match between my school and a visiting team I succeeded in knocking over the stumps three t
imes by mistake, sending a tray of tea over the gown of the Headmaster's wife and sitting on a gentleman's top hat.

Every week I appeared to do something to amuse the other boys unintentionally. Then came the day when I left, the final prize-giving day. I excelled myself in clumsiness. I was being awarded a minor prize of a book. When my name was called I jumped to my feet and tried to stroll nonchalantly towards the table where the books were piled. Alas it was as if I were a marionette and someone else pulled the strings. As I stretched out my hand to receive my prize, my little finger caught the fringe of the table cloth and as I tried to wrench it free I only succeeded in pulling the cloth, sending the pile of books scattering on the floor, followed by a carafe of water and a glass. A cascade of water trickled over the books like a miniature Niagara and there I stood with the wretched cloth still attached to my finger as if joined for eternity by the tassled fringe."

Percival rambled on in this manner, filling pages with his misfortunes as a junior clerk, seeking female companionship and eventually meeting Mathilda, the local undertaker's daughter. He proposed and was accepted by the young lady who had a spotty skin, a large nose and protruding teeth like a rabbit. I pick up his story on the wedding day ...

"Was the sun shining? Were the birds singing? No. An unearthly silence in a world stilled by thick yellow fog. Would nothing go right? I arrived at the church early with my best man, the guests started to arrive and gradually the church became a seething mass of impatient bodies. As is the custom the bride was late, but alas it was not just to satisfy convention.

When she eventually sailed up the aisle I noticed with dismay that it was not the bouquet of roses she had talked about for weeks, but a posy of china flowers as found under glass upon graves, while her two bridesmaids each carried three waxen lilies which I knew graced the desk in the funeral parlour. These they held like pokers ready to assault the first person they met. Of course the explanation was that the florist had been held up in the fog and instead of doing without flowers these funeral tokens were Mathilda's answer.

Then came the ring. My best man had it safe, but upon it being laid on the prayer book it rolled off and a harassed clergyman, best man and bridegroom were banging their heads together to retrieve it. So the service continued with horror upon horror as the bride's knuckles had swollen owing to her shutting her finger in a drawer while adorning herself and the ring would only go halfway down her finger.

So we were wed. The banquet that followed was but a cold collation, the speeches were the usual nonsense spoken at all weddings, until it was my turn and I was in such confusion that I caught my breath, had a fit of coughing and spilled the champagne. At last we left for our honeymoon and of course the train was over an hour late.

We arrived at a seafront hotel and I will not dwell upon our wedding night which is best forgotten. Next day my troubles continued but my wife just laughed as I so often tried to perform a simple task and ended up with a mess.

The sun shone brightly for this time of autumn so we decided on a long walk. Although Mathilda was getting tired we climbed further. Upon reaching the woods we decided to rest and to our horror Mathilda discovered she had lost her wedding ring. Oh dear, the next few hours were spent searching, but in vain. In fact the rest of our honeymoon was spent in retracing our steps and searching. However, we left at the end of our stay two very sad people who had wasted so much time looking for a golden ring.

We even returned to the Island for the next three years before giving up our search. The tragic experience had spoilt our marriage. Can you who hears me look for the ring as I can see it now and may be able to light up your way. I can see myself as a

Some of the many artefacts which have been discovered.

huge joke and if I could have laughed at myself then life would have been more fun. Find the ring and think of us both and laugh."

For the next half an hour Wally and I scrambled over the stones and rough ground, first one side of the wall, then the other. Just as I was about to say it was hopeless Walter climbed over the broken wall and as he did so I saw a shaft of light pass right through him. I told him to stand still as that must be the place. Wally stood motionless and I picked my way to him.

We both looked down and there alongside the wall lay a golden ring. A tree had begun to grow through it, the seed must have fallen into the centre of the ring and now the tiny oak was encircled by it. There arose from the earth a living finger wearing the ring.

*   *   *

Whether the haunting is in the wild or within walls, most ghosts speak of a passage or brilliant light suddenly appearing to offer them release, and this must be the same as that witnessed by those who have had Near Death Experiences. Evidently this passage is not permanently open and if not taken immediately it disappears, leaving the person earthbound. Some ghosts have told me how they had gone half-way through then turned back, only to find the passage closing behind them, and they too became trapped.

Not all ghosts enjoy the same freedom of movement once stuck. Some find themselves limited to a small area of ground or within the boundaries of a house; others can move a greater distance but only between set limits. However, there are some who suffer a worse fate, for I have come across a dozen or so ghosts attached to objects, helpless. One such case involved a teetotal clergyman transported into a busy pub. It was not so much a release for him, more a rescue from Hell.

*   *   *

The ghostly Larry wasn't so much found in the wild, more in the rough – of the seventh hole of the Ventnor golf course. I include this case and the next because these two ghosts provided some tantalising clues as to what lies beyond the famous tunnel of light, and prove that for many becoming earthbound is far from accidental:

"They called me Larry. My name is Lawrence. I put on all the airs and graces I thought my name demanded. I joined the golf club when it first opened and enjoyed a game twice a week; it was an expensive hobby. The fellow players thought I had money, I drove a small shiny respectable car, lived in a small respectable house among respectable neighbours.

What no-one knew except my wife was that we were broke. We lived very frugally and my wife had a cleaning job away from where we lived and I did night work as well as a day job, four nights a week. No-one knew of this. My money went on golf; my wife and children suffered and she pleaded with me to give up this expensive hobby. I would not. I was so selfish.

When I died I saw how old my wife had become, although she was only forty-three; my children looked pinched and hungry. I was in my fifties. I have had to stay for some time. 'Since you love golf so much you can stay with it,' some woman said, I do not know who. I have been here for years, now by confessing I see an opening and shall go on to where golf is not played. Thank you for helping me."

So there you have it. Golf is not played in heaven.

There was no 'find' with Larry, though I did come across an old golf ball in the place where he had waited on the orders of some female being beyond the tunnel of light; but it was Jake who provided a description of sorts of those who had condemned him to his ghostly fate. Jake was found haunting some rough ground near Osborne House in East Cowes.

"They called me Jake. I was here to help with the building; was not paid much. Had five nippers to feed. The wife nagged a lot for more money, so I stole from the master builder. Ten shillings it were. 'E caught me and 'it me on the jaw, broke two teeth. I got even with 'im, left the ladder in 'is way; 'e tripped, broke 'is arm. I was not sorry. I blamed it on old Tom who also helped with the stonework. Tom 'ad money stopped from 'is wage for what 'e didn't do.

When I died I could not go on. I caused an accident and stole. Old Tom got the push and never 'ad no job again and nearly starved to death. Strange women said I 'ad to stop 'ere. Now I can go on through a tunnel to the light. 'Ope I reach the light at the end. Who were these women? Not angels, they wore hoods."

CHAPTER SIX

THE SEA, THE MAID AND THE DYING POET

I WAS AT home polishing the table when I first heard Lizzie's voice. On many occasions over the following three months, and usually when I was least expecting it, she would interrupt me in my household chores. I welcomed these interruptions as I soon developed an affection for her gentle Island accent and would write down all she said. It would only be a few sentences at a time, but little by little Lizzie confided in me of her secret love for the great English poet, John Keats.

Lizzie, it seems, may have deprived English literature of an ode by Keats, an ode with a strange and sad coincidence concerning the death of another famous poet of the age. John Keats had visited the Island three times during his short and tragic life. The first was in the spring of 1817, at the beginning of his career, when he had left the dirty air of London to be alone with his poetry. He had lodged near Carisbrooke Castle, and brought with him his favourite books and shared a room with a bust of Shakespeare. Keats was twenty-two at that time and from the many letters which have survived him it is clear the poetry of love and beauty filled him with such intensity he could barely sleep at nights.

While on the Island he was composing his thoughts, preparing a poem of the young man Endymion and his search for the goddess of the Moon. The sea fascinated Keats, and the picturesque scenery around the east of the Island charmed him with "wood and meadow and cliffs and clefts filled with trees and bushes and primroses which spread to the very verge of the sea".

Two years later, in the summer of 1819, Keats returned and this time he chose to stay in that pretty place he remembered; but much had changed for the poet during that short time. The 'bower of youth' had been rubbed raw by harsh experience, he had lost his two brothers who were so very close to him; one emigrated to America, the other dead from consumption – a disease Keats knew might claim him. Already he suffered from a sore throat which had complicated into a much worse condition and was the reason for his convalescence on the Island.

51

It was a wretched time. The climate was not kind and bad weather brought damp air to aggravate his condition. He did not stay in isolation this time, he was accompanied by his friend, a man named Rice who also suffered chronic ill-health. Instead of revitalising him, as Keats so desperately hoped, the visit to the Island actually made him feel worse and even more melancholy.

Even the picturesque had lost its charm for the poet, and he declared he could only now enjoy its beauty through the eyes of another. Keats, who had always been more dedicated to his work than chasing women, had found his beloved – Fanny Brawne. But already it was too late, for as their love grew he knew his body weakened and always, always the fear that consumption would take hold, eat away his breath, his life and with it his love.

Many believe some of the world's finest poetry was borne of the ebb and flow of that young man's suffering. He was only twenty-four.

The picturesque may have lost its charm for Keats, but not the sea its fascination. At first I had no idea to whom Lizzie was referring, so I just listened and wrote what was said; but each day she confided in me, growing more bold as she spoke of her theft from the man staying at the Shanklin cottage where she was the maid. 'Impossible love' is such a feature of Keats' life and poetry – even when he was not aware of it; for there was also Lizzie's love, just as impossible.

"... The poor man was not well. The Missus says to see his bed is aired. I took the warming pan up to his room. Poor man was coughing real bad. He was only here to stay for a while. Very kind at first. Spoke nice too.

I had never see so pretty a gentleman, such pale skin. I wanted to touch his hands. He spoke softly and used such lovely words. He was writing poetry most of the time. I had to creep around so as not to disturb him. I wished he would notice me.

The cottage where I worked was on the cliff with a view of the sea. That's why the lovely man stayed there. He kept saying how beautiful it was, and something about uplifting his soul. He talked funny sometimes. One day he sat in the garden writing and I left my jobs in the house and sat near him. I could not stop looking at him. He was not well and kept coughing. I was scolded for not scouring the pots properly. I wanted to see what he was writing. I was only a simple young servant but I fell in love with him and his lovely way of talking. The nice young man was in love with someone called Fanny. She lived far from here. Ma said I be stupid to think of him. He kept coughing. His friend was with him and called him John. I did something bad while he was out walking. I went into his room and took a piece of what he was writing. I could not read it but kept it for a long time, all my life. I learnt to read and write so as I be able to see what it says. Ma said I be very bad. I never loved no other man like that nice John who used funny words like odes and things.

The nice John was asking his friend if he had seen his notes. He said it was not important, but he wondered where he had put them. I knew. I had folded it carefully and put it in my bodice while I swept the kitchen floor. He asked me if I had seen it, but I told a lie. I took it home. I be very happy I have something his own hand had writted and I slept with it under my pillow that night. I be wishing his cough was better.

I kept the writing for a long time before I knew what it said. I was frightened to ask anybody to read it to me. Then an old man who lived near Ma and me said he would learn me to read if I would help him with his cabbages. It took a long time but I did learn and then I could read his lovely words. If they had been of his love for me I could not have loved them more, but it was what he called notes to his friend. I be so glad to have them and read them a lot. They says ..."

I heard Lizzie take a breath and in her soft Island voice speak the words she had stolen ...

"'The sea was so calm yesterday I threw a pebble and watched the ripples growing wider and wider. My thoughts wandered. Today the sea is so rough. Ode To A Wave. O white crested wave in foam-flecked sea. Would anyone be interested? No-one but Fanny. Does she know how I pine for her? Foam-flecked sea with white crested waves ...'

That was one bit of his writing but I loved it and kept reading it with the other bits:

'Ah gentle wave doth thou caress the shore with a lover's kiss.'

That was a bit of the writing I liked best. I let Ma see it but she could not read. This writing is smaller than how I learnt. I wished he could have stayed longer. The Missus did not know about the notes, she would have beaten me. Ma says I be very wicked but I love the waves and sometimes go to the seashore to watch them. I be very glad he write what he did. One morning he stopped and talked to me. I shall always think of what he said.

There was a bit of writing I did not like much, so as it was at the bottom of the page I tore it off as it was not any happy lines:

'O angry wave like a Titan in shroud
On destructive course watched o'er by dark cloud.'

˙ It made me tremble because it made me think of dying and the nice man looks white and ill and his cough be bad. The Missus gave I a pretty box she did not want anymore and it be my birthday. It had a painted flower on the lid so I kept Mister Keats' writing in it.

It were nigh on two years 'fore I could make out what it said, then I tore the bit off the bottom. He had looked so bad when he left I wondered if he had ever got better. I asked the Missus if she ever heard but she says I had to get on with me scrubbing.

One day I watched him in the garden writing and I peeked to see what the writing looked like, but I did not understand it. He asked me to fetch something from his room. That was the only time he spoke to me. When I gave him it, he says 'Have any men told you that your eyes are like grey pebbles in the moonlight?' I never forgot that, it were lovely. I looked in the looking-glass that Ma had, lots of times at my eyes after that. Ma says I be wicked.

The Missus said I must take up water to fill Mister Keats' jug and as I put it in the jug I saw a pile of papers lying there. I be so bad. Seeing them I took the top piece. It were a long time before I be able to see what it says, silly sort of bits really, but I loved them. The first bit was about Ode to a wave and foam flecked sea. I know what he means, and then he put:

'The sea is too restless to write about. No ode could do it justice. One day so calm with the reflected sunlight dancing like a million diamonds; the next so rough with Titan-sized waves.'

I likes the sea. Sometimes I walk along the shore. It be lovely on a hot day it be. The Missus says I should pay more attention to seeing the pots are well-scrubbed.

'O ever changing sea, never the same
Doth thou enjoy drowning the unwary?'

I like this bit of Mister Keats' writing. When I was in bed at night and heard the waves I thought of this. I likes to hear the big waves when I be safe in Ma's cottage with me shawl wrapped around me. Not like who he writ about:

'Unwary sailor caught in thy grasp.'

Poor man, him so ill, coughing and worrying about a sailor drowning. I be glad I got his writings.

I wished my name be Fanny. He kept on about her to his friend who stayed with him. He said he felt such an ache in his heart for her. The kitchen door was open a crack and I could hear what they be talking about. He said he wished his heart was as tranquil as the sea. I does not know what he did mean, but it sounded nice and the sun was warm and birds singing. I went home to Ma and asked her why she had not called I Fanny. She said I be that bad. I asked Ma what tranquil meant, but she did not know. It sounds nice the way he said it, and he said:

'Tranquillity be thy name today mad sea.'

I cried for three days and nights after John Keats had left. Ma said I be that stupid to love someone not of me own kind. 'Old Barnes' son be looking your way,' she says but how could I think of that thick-headed boy when I thinks of the lovely words Mister Keats used? I may be stupid, but I know how it felt to love deeply.

Sometimes wherever he be I hoped he thought of a stupid girl with eyes like pebbles in the moonlight. The full moon after he left I went to the shore to look at a pebble in the moonlight. It shone pretty-like. This bit of writing be on the back of the notes:

'Vain cloud like Narcissus gazing from the sky
Restless waves disturbing thy reflection.'

I always would think of clouds over the sea as vain. Ma said I be vain when I look in her looking-glass. I always wished I be having blue eyes, but after what he said I be ever so glad they be grey. Ma said Mister Keats must be a clever gentleman to know the words he do.

'Doth Zephyrus sing above thee O wave?'

I be wishing I knew what he meant. Even the old man who learnt I to read did not know. Said it were something foreign.

'Moonlight on dwelling place of Proteus
Enchantment. Enchanting. Ench . . .'

That bit did not finish. Sometimes he has the look of someone far away, as if he lives in a dream, yet he be so clever. His hands be that white and soft. I could not help seeing when I gave him the book he asked me to fetch. He would not be a strong man, not like the men here with brown hard hands, all scars and bumps.

I be sweeping when Mister Rice left. He put three pence in my hand and said 'You are a good girl Lizzie.' He would not have said that if he knew I took the notes, but I be pleased to get three whole pence to meself. I spent it on some ribbon which I tied around the box I keept the notes of nice John in and gave Ma one pence for herself too.

It be silly to worry over the sea if you be not going out in a boat, I thinks. But Mister Keats kept onto his friend how he must write about the sea or the waves before he left. I knows he wrote such a lot and had his notes hidden away in me pretty box. He kept saying he had a good line there. I be not knowing what he meant. Ma says I be wicked. I nearly put it back on his table as he told his friend he could not remember. But I could not as it be silly to worry over the sea to write about and I be wanting to keept his writing for ever.

Old man Barnes told I that he be talking to nice Mister Keats. Said he were a fine young gentleman but was too pale in the face. Said he be asking about the sea and what it be like in a fishing boat when the waves be so big. Old man Barnes told I he has been all morning wandering on shore talking to them down there. He be that interested in how high the waves be when it be winter storms, old man Barnes said. I wondered if he would ever come back here in the winter to see. I had hoped so but it be but a dream as he never did.

The Missus had made a petticoat and I swept up the pieces of pale blue sarsenet off the floor. She said I could took them if I be wanting them. I took them and lined the pretty box she did give I and the lovely John's paper would not be spoilt and could lay on the soft bed I had made for ever. It be like the blue of the sea when the sun shines on it, lovely blue. Ma says I be bad.

The Missus said I need not work on the Sunday but could go to church. After church I ran back to her cottage to see if she be wanting any pots scoured.

I be wishing to see him. She said to get along home. I think she knew how I felt. I did not see him and cried that night. Ma says I be bad."

*   *   *

During the time Lizzie spoke to me I was fortunate enough to visit the cottage. In one hundred and seventy years not so much had changed, although at one time it had been partly demolished. It had since returned to being a hotel. The rooms, however, are largely the same with the only real modifications being a door here and there bricked over.

Keats' room is at the back of the building, facing south, its windows spaced together like two eyes looking seaward. The view has since become obscured by modern building, hotels mostly. The landlord seemed accustomed to strangers visiting to see the poet's room and was obliging enough to talk over what he knew and show what features remained and what had changed. Biographers and various literary historians have come to experience the room and try to imagine the scene.

As I sat in the little room I sensed a presence and heard a sad sigh. I believe it was Lizzie and I felt tears in my eyes. As I wiped them away I found myself in a different arrangement. The manager who had been talking faded, as did his words; the wallpaper had changed to a cream colour with pale blue and red pattern. I found myself sitting in the doorway – now bricked over – beside the fireplace. Nearby stood a small table with a white tablecloth on which I could see a china wash bowl and white towel draped over the side. On the other side of the fireplace was another small table on which stood a tray and a plate with the remnants of a meal. I know always these experiences are over almost as quickly as they begin, they are just flashes but long enough to take in quite a lot of information so I looked around while I had the chance.

In the far corner opposite the window stood a four-poster bed without curtains; in another corner a rocking chair with an uncomfortable-looking red cushion. On the bare wooden floor lay a rug with a red border and pale blue pattern. Then something caught my eye, a movement. Across the room was a large table at which sat a figure. He had not moved until that moment, but he shifted and threw something which bounced off the table and onto the floor by his right foot. The figure wore a black coat and had his back to me; but I watched as he bent over and picked up the fallen object and then returned it to the table-top. I saw it was a quill, but now useless

57

Keats' Cottage, Shanklin.

as the man took another from the left-hand side of the table. As he shifted his position I could see a brass-topped inkwell and by his right elbow an untidy pile of papers. He wrote a few words and then stopped. He picked up a small silver knife from beside the oil lamp, sharpened the new quill and continued writing.

Next thing I knew the landlord was talking about some television programme and I was back. It had happened in a fraction of an instant. Would I care to see the rest of the house? he asked, and I think I nodded for him to lead on.

I was shown the rest of the lodging-house, through the upstairs bedroom, presumably where the man Rice had slept; and downstairs into what is now the family sitting room. The memory of the scene in the upstairs bedroom haunted me as I followed the manager, listening vaguely to what he was saying. I remembered a description of Keats' face from a woman who had met him when the young poet was filled with the inspiration of beauty and love, before the onset of his illness.

A man with large blue eyes and auburn hair which he wore divided down the centre so it fell in rich masses on each side of his face. "His countenance one of singular beauty and brightness, it had an expression as if he had been looking on some glorious sight. The shape of his face had not the squareness of a man's, but more like some woman's face, so wide over the forehead and so small at the chin."*

I thought of the figure bent over the desk. The illness no doubt must have affected his appearance, but still he stirred the heart of the simple maid who gazed so lovingly upon those features. The manager invited me into the sitting room and I felt I could not be certain which century I was in, for where the son of the family was laying across the plush sofa reading a newspaper amid the trappings of modern entertainments there was a squalid little room with wooden settle, a dresser stacked with ornaments and jars, and a bed with a patchwork quilt. Where there now stands a plush red carpet I saw a brown dingy rug and a circular table surrounded by chairs and in the centre of the table an oil lamp. Then the vision faded and I was being steered towards the kitchen.

I found myself staring at an early nineteenth-century kitchen complete with hip bath and buckets, warming pans and oil lamps and a large wooden table in the centre of the room. I noticed something move in front of a brass candlestick and could hear the

[*Quoted in *The Life and Letters of John Keats*. Lord Houghton, Everyman's Library.]

manager tapping his fingertips against a glass panel explaining that it was the original glass. I rubbed my eyes and saw a modern kitchen, but strangely enough a shadow was there, where the candlesticks had stood before.

It was a ghost and it had latched onto me. It was impossible to write so I had to wait until I was outside before I could attend to it. The tour was over anyway and so I thanked the manager for his time and made my exit. The ghost became more insistent I attend to him so I found a seat nearby and waited. Then I heard the voice of a young man:

"Brought milk from the farm every day. The Missus or the young girl came out with a big jug. I was a handsome man, thought the Missus a comely woman, red-faced with hands that could do anything I thought. The girl was sweet but a little simple, she could never remember whether to bring the white jug or a patterned one. Kept getting scolded. She lived in a dream.

I cheated on the milk everytime it was her, never quite filled the jug. Couldn't do this if it were the Missus that came out. She would have given me a clip round the ears. I often went into the cottage for a slice of apple pie if she were out. I would take extra if the girl was looking elsewhere, 'specially if a young man was in the garden. I spent a lot of time idling away time in that cottage. Stole money from a pot on the ledge over the stove.

Sometimes the girl was blamed, or the boy who did odd jobs once a week. It never troubled me. I was not honest, relied on my charming smile that would turn any head. I was like this at other cottages. Stole, gave less milk and drank far too much at the inn. I was hurt by a rusty nail, it turned nasty and got a fever. Came back here.

Was it the comely woman, the simple girl or the apple pie? I do not understand, but can now travel along a road of light towards heaven, or the woman, or the girl? I do not know, but you who lives now helps me. Thankyou. I am tired of delivering milk in the cart."

Lizzie did not speak again for a while after that and I wondered what had happened. In fact I began to miss the sound of her voice. Somehow I knew the story had not concluded, but Lizzie did not wish to communicate.

Perhaps it was coincidence, perhaps not, but several days later I decided to visit the little church near the cottage. It is a pretty place, and Keats had often visited it with his friend Charles Brown who came to stay after Rice's departure. The church is very old and stands a half mile from the cottage, on the lower slopes of the hills above the town. I sat in the pews in the cool musty interior of the church and listened, hoping for something, anything. Sure enough the familiar and gentle voice of Lizzie whispered close to my ear.

"The vicar had preached for a long time, something about loving thy neighbour. It be so hot in church. I be watching the lady in the front with the lovely bonnet of flowers on. She had a fan. I be praying for the nice John to talk to me. I ran back to the cottage. He was not there. Missus did not want me, she had a friend with her. Ma says I be bad."

Lizzie paused and I heard her sigh.

"When I got wedded I thought of him and wondered what it be like to be touched with soft hands like his be. My man had rough hands. I always thought of him and after I were learnt to read I often read his writing and I kept the box with it hidden

St Blasius Church, Shanklin.

behind a loose brick in the back room. I be not wanting my man to see it ever.

I be so happy with my clothes. If I had not had respectable ones Mister Keats might not have seen me eyes. The lady who stayed with the Missus before he gave me a bonnet she had finished with, so I wore it every day instead of me old cotton cap when he was there. It were dark but I put bright ribbons on and Missus said I looked as if I was trying to ape my betters. I did not know what she meant but I wanted to look nice for him.

He seemed sad most of the time, but one morning I heard him singing softly to himself. Not very well mind but it showed he was a bit happy. Ma says I be bad. Dear God let Mister Keats return. I will be so good and not make anyone cross with me. I be loving him so much. The Barnes boy came a-calling last night and Brown the night before. Please God let him come back. Amen."

There was a long silence and I thought it was over and so gathered myself ready to leave when I heard her voice again.

"'Man that is born of woman hath but a short time to live,' the vicar said. Poor Ma. She said I be bad and now she has gone. He has never returned and I 'spect he has gone too. Please God let me see him in heaven when I be dead. Amen."

As she finished I looked up from writing and there stood a figure in front of the altar. She was looking upwards, her head thrown back. She wore a long pale grey dress, a grey shawl with a black fringe over her shoulders and a faded black poke bonnet on her head. I am no artist but I quickly drew a rough pencil sketch of the figure, which I painted when I returned home . She was visible for only about three minutes before she faded. Lizzie never spoke again.

Many who have read the lines Lizzie stole have since agreed they are just as Keats wrote. I have often wondered about the wooden box but no doubt her cottage, along with many others, has long gone to make way for a modern hotel or a block of flats. The box would not have protected the paper inside against rotting and presumably they are now dust, crumbled and flattened by building. Treasures lost and therefore cannot be authenticated as being by the poet's hand. Yet not really, for they live on to those who listen to the words of love from a sweet simple girl named Lizzie.

Sketch of Lizzie in Shanklin church, June 1977.

The poet did return during the winter. Well nearly. John Keats lay on board a ship anchored off the shore of the Island. It was one year later and Keats was bound for the warm climate of Italy, a journey he hoped would help him live. He was desperately ill with consumption and knew he was dying. He was leaving behind his love, his friends and unbeknown to him the little maid Lizzie.

John Keats died in Rome on the morning of the 23rd February 1821. As a man he is remembered with great affection in literary history, not simply for his character and courage, but because he was one of the great poets, a brilliant star in the constellation which included Wordsworth, Byron and of course Shelley.

It is some small coincidence that one year later the body of Percy Bysse Shelley was recovered from the sea off the coast of Italy. He had drowned while sailing. In his pocket was found a book of poems, the poems of John Keats.

CHAPTER SEVEN

WHO'S SORRY NOW?

WHEN I set forth on a journey to release a ghost I never know what will happen, the story I shall hear nor what I may be led to find. All I need is a car to get me to the haunted place, a paper and pencil, and some helpers. There is not always a 'find' as I call it with every ghost, but sometimes there is.

Identifying a ghost by way of confirming their name and lifetime through historical document is always a good source of proof; but nothing can compare with the moment when we are led to some lonely place and a ghost speaks their sorry confession and tells of something important in their lives, then shows us where that thing lays buried beneath the soil. When that very object is unearthed, it is then that I and all those with me know the truth of it all – that ghosts exist.

I never work alone and all sorts of people have accompanied me on these releases; even a film camera team, whose astonishment was evident on their faces by the end of those days filming. During the time they filmed me there was a ghost haunting the cliffs of Brook beach, on the west of the Island. The director, cameraman and sound engineer followed me down to the beach and along in the direction of Freshwater; then, having sensed the ghost, I stopped and tried to stall him from speaking while the camera team set up their equipment. Some minutes later all was ready; the director whispered and pointed to the cameraman, then held his breath. The camera was rolling and I let the ghost speak:

"I used to take bets from the chaps as to which pretty girl I could get a date with. Sometimes I lost, but not always. I was so charming and good-looking. One day they bet me I would not take Babs for a date. She was ugly and wore thick-lensed glasses. The money they wagered was good so I took it on and the poor soul was thrilled to be asked out. We went to a pub and then I took advantage. She was easy. I then took her out once more just for a dare. I dropped her when she tried to make advances herself. Some months later I had a message asking me to meet her out on the cliffs above you. She lived somewhere here nearby. I thought I would.

When I met her she first gave me a little gift saying I was a king-like man and thought this was suitable; then said she was three months gone with my child and I must marry her. 'You have to Bert,' she said. I panicked, and looked at the tiny thing in my hand. Threw it over the cliffs and pushed her away. She slipped and fell over the cliffs; she lost the child because of this and was ill for ages. I never saw her again, went overseas; but realised how beastly I had behaved. I died and came back here. Now you can help me onwards. You can find it. It is up above you, you will have to climb. It is there. I can see it. Thankyou. Can go on now."

The camera was rolling as I read back the message and began the work of finding the object. The cliff is broken in that area and requires much care to climb; but the wind was strong and got inside my coat and puffed me up like a balloon while the cameraman followed me and Nicholas, who was with us that day, around the piles of earth. I had no idea what it might be, "a gift for a king-like man," but he'd said it was tiny. It was after some time of searching when at last Nicholas found in a crack in the ground a small golden-coloured bracelet charm in the shape of a throne.

It was quite an amazing experience when later we watched the whole event being played back on the screen, and the moment of discovery. David, Robin and his son Danny accompanied me on several further releases and admitted how the experience had changed their understanding, and even their lives.

This ghost work does seem to have that effect on people, and now I often have phonecalls from those who have been out with me on a release asking for more work; some think of it as doing a good deed to help a soul, others come along for the 'finds' we discover. Indeed we have unearthed a strange collection of objects, even one day a sari.

This too was found near Brook, though this time it was near the church above the village. We had driven out for the day and having been inside the church decided to follow a nearby path for a better view of the strange grey mansion on the hilltop above. The path was well overgrown with nettles and brambles and after a while it was such difficult going that we decided to turn back. Nearing the church I suddenly came to a stop – something was near me. Then a voice, breathless:

"Cor blimey, I 'ad to run and catch you. Why didn't you stay and go a little 'igher than you did?"

I hastily grabbed my paper and pencil as he spoke on.

"I was born in the east end of London, married an Indian girl when working in Bombay. Brought 'er 'ome. Said she must give up wearin' saris, wanted her to look more English like. She 'ad lovely dark eyes and I loved 'er, but 'ated saris. She said she 'ad given 'em all away; but when we came 'ere on 'oliday I found one in 'er case, 'er favourite.

I got real nasty. 'Scum,' I said, called 'er awful names; took scissors and in front of 'er cut it in 'alf. Cor blimey you should 'ave 'eard the row. She said she 'ad always 'ated me, used me to get to England. We went back to London, separated and then I 'eard she 'ad died. I was so sad. Real upset I were, and then I was looking in a case and found the sari I 'ad cut in 'alf. I felt sorry, so made a pilgrimage to this church that was our last place of 'appiness before the big row.

I prayed for forgiveness and I put the pieces wrapped up near the place where you climbed just now, but 'igher. I was dead by the end of the month of an illness I brought on meself and I found meself back guarding them pieces so as they never get wet. Please find 'em. I am going as I 'ave told me tale. David is me name, David 'enry. Please remember me as I go through a path of green and silver sparkling. Thanks, 'oping you will find 'em."

I read what I had heard and we turned back up the path and pushed on further through the nettles and brambles, beyond where we had first turned back, and on the left-hand side I saw a weak glint of silver light on the ground and pointed out the spot in the middle of a nettle patch.

Walter was with me that day and stamped back the nettles and set about digging and it wasn't long before he pulled something from the ground. It looked like a rolled-up filthy sock, and soaking wet. He passed it to me and I unrolled it and found inside a dirty piece of wrapping and inside that was a piece of cloth, a sea green colour with pretty patterns of coloured sequins.

Unfortunately in some places the damp had penetrated the wrapping as there were faded patches. I held it up and saw it was jaggedly cut, while Wally searched the ground and found another filthy sock nearby and pulled that out and unrolled the contents. It was the other half. Together the two pieces became a beautiful sari; the wrapping had protected it reasonably well, but left much longer it would have been completely ruined.

The author with the sari discovered near Brook Church.

Having worked with ghosts for so long it might be a strange thing to say, but their existence scares me. Not in the way most people might think – I am not afraid *of* ghosts, but more fearful *because* of them. What frightens me most is how easy it is to become one. This is the truly scary thing. No-one is perfect. Who hasn't done something worthy of regret?

Harriet could not have found much company where she was haunting – high up on a steep hillside of Brighstone Downs. There are no houses around for miles and it is not a place often visited and, despite its lovely view, it is a lonely spot.

The sun was shining and there was still warmth in the rays on that afternoon in early autumn when we found Harriet. After a walk of about one mile we had to scramble over some rough ground to reach the haunted area and came to a halt on a steep slope. It was an uncomfortable place to sit and wait, and I watched a group of butterflies as they danced their final dances of the year. I felt someone close:

"...Mamma had said to gain the attention of a gentleman one had to appear interested in all he said, and sometimes join in his pastimes. I liked Mister Cameron, a gentleman with plenty of money, from Scotland. He showed great interest in me and as he called at the house on many occasions it was hoped he would declare himself. I did find some of his conversation a little boring, but would not show it. One of these was his interest in Roman history. We came up here as he had heard Roman remains had been discovered in this vicinity.

We came in two small traps – Lucy my friend, James and Charlotte my brother and sister, and aunt Emily came as chaperone. Mister Cameron found a piece of pottery which excited him. I wandered around here poking the ground with a stick and to my joy found a Roman coin. This would make Mister Cameron realise what an excellent wife I would be, I was thinking as I started to return to the others. As I went around a bush I saw him kissing Lucy.

I quickly poked the coin back into the earth. I then ran towards my aunt and informed her that Mister Cameron had interfered with me. Find the coin as it is near where you are and I will tell you what happened. Then I can continue towards the light."

It was difficult to keep our balance up on that hillside. I dropped my pencil and it rolled downhill. Wally and Doreen both tried to grab it and banged their heads together. There were shrieks of laughter from her but Wally was rubbing his head and looking angrily at me. The hard chalky earth did not make for easy digging and we only had garden trowels, but eventually we found the spot and uncovered a Roman coin. It was in poor condition, but that did not matter as the thrill of finding an artefact always makes me happy.

I sat down again and waited for Harriet to speak.

"...I was so wicked telling such a lie. Mister Cameron denied touching me. My friend said he had only been with her a matter of minutes so could not verify his remarks. We all returned home. I was crying as I was so disappointed seeing him kiss another while my lips ached for his kisses. Not one had he ever bestowed on me. All the time I had been listening to his boring conversation about the Romans. I said he pulled up my skirt and, oh I blush to think what else he was supposed to have done. All lies, but the poor man was ruined forever. His reputation in shreds.

He returned to his native Scotland and was not heard of again. I was ruined also as these lies were believed and did my reputation no good. No-one was interested in a girl who had been defiled by another man, even if it was all lies. How are they to know?

I died an old maid and found myself wandering around here, guarding the coin until it was found. My story is told and a silver light shines forth. I shall go towards it. My name is Harriet, thank you for helping me."

And Harriet was gone. The three of us were exhausted and there was still the long walk back to the car. Doreen was looking somewhat dishevelled and yet she was still smiling; Wally was examining the coin and I felt happy as I always do after releasing a ghost. Some releases are difficult and tiring, but that passes; and I know that Harriet is no longer haunting that lonely hillside, remembering over and over an old coin and a kiss that never was.

Coming across coins and rings in this work is common enough (although I've not so far found any caches of gold coins), but I now have quite a collection of unusual objects; there are plates, cups, spoons, statues, and all manner of jewellery and ornaments (although again nothing precious in material terms). The largest of course is the sari which I have kept. I have also an ivy-shaped dish claimed to have once belonged to the famous Florrie Ford.* This was found in the Landslip between Ventnor and Shanklin. The area has changed much since, for as the name suggests it is a place of landslip; but on that day Barbara, Walter and I followed one of the old paths which led to Bonchurch when all of a sudden I was

[*The celebrated Australian-born Music Hall singer best remembered for her performances of *Down At The Old Bull And Bush* and, during the First World War, *Pack Up Your Troubles In Your Old Kit Bag.*]

stopped. I had the feeling as if there was a hand on my chest compelling me to stop. Often there is this feeling when I come across a ghost. The others settled quietly while I listened:

"The man I worked for was a funny man. Said he chose me from lots of women who wanted the job, 'cause my name is Florrie. He had met Florrie Ford, the Music Hall singer; he had done some work for her, don't know what.

She gave him a dish like the ivy. He was always at the piano playing 'Just Like The Ivy'. Had to polish the dish, ash tray I said it was. One lady said it was a vine leaf, they rowed over this. Had to polish the blasted thing every day. One day he said my work wasn't being done well enough, always in a rush to get home. I smashed a couple of plates, a clock and tore a shirt when ironing it. That got me into more trouble.

I got so angry I took his prize possession, his ivy dish. Never thought Florrie Ford really did give him the dish. I threw it away when out here for a walk. You can find it down the bank behind you to prove I am real. I died four years later and had to stay here. I was so bad, doing much wilful damage. Find it, then I can go on and meet the man who I worked for and tell him it is safe, as he has gone on. Please find it. I see a bright light. Thank you."

It did not take long to find the dish. Barbara found it.

* * *

As the months and years have passed, the more artefacts have been unearthed, and each has a ghost attached with a sorry tale to tell. All those who have taken part in this work and have witnessed the discoveries, or even themselves pulled the objects out of the ground, now believe ghosts exist. Indeed it is a dangerous misconception to think there is no such thing, for their very presence serves to remind us all that it seems we are expected to account for our actions when our lives are ended – remember the ghostly golfer Lawrence, and the "hooded women" met by Jake – and that is a scary thought.

Being a religious official does not seem to assure anyone of a guaranteed fast-track to heavenly bliss, however much they might wish it so; for I have plenty of clergymen of every denomination amongst my case files and even Archbishops have been found stuck haunting the cathedrals of Britain. There is the saying "Our sins will come back to haunt us"; perhaps it is better to say "We come back to haunt our sins". If you've wronged someone, best try to right it while you can. It's not much fun being a ghost.

More of the many artefacts which have been discovered.

CHAPTER EIGHT

THE MARY ROSE

A MONGST THE brick buildings and cranes and grey city-ships of
Portsmouth dockyard can be found some famous old boats.
The *Victory* is a magnificent sight; she stands perched and
preened in her warpaint of black and gold, and bristling with guns.
Beside her rests an elder sister, the *Mary Rose*, once the pride of King
Henry VIII's battlefleet, though now a semi-skeleton preserved in a
shed.

The *Mary Rose* had lain on the seabed for 437 years; over the
centuries anchors and lines had dragged away half her timbers, but
the rest were buried into the seabed and there preserved and her
exact whereabouts long forgotten. Then one day the sands parted to
reveal the exposed ribs of the ship. The fish watched the activity as
they did every day, and when one morning in 1981 the wreck site was
swarming with divers, even the crabs backed deep into the crevices
between the old planks and feelered their defiance. Unbeknown to
the creatures was the reason for all the extra activity, for in the midst
of the divers was a royal in a rubber suit, the Prince Charles.

After the experience the Prince offered his observations. "I was
swimming along quite happily poking around when I looked down
into a hole; suddenly I came face to face with a skull. I must say it did
give me quite a fright," said he, "... this skull marvellously preserved,
beautiful teeth, absolutely perfect."* The following year the *Mary Rose*
was plucked from beneath the mud, oil and sewage of the Solent and
brought home to the dockyard.

In fact there were hundreds of bones, the best part of seven
hundred sets scattered around the wreck. The *Mary Rose* wasn't just
a wreck, she was a disaster; and it happened right in front of big
Henry, below his very nose. The *Mary Rose* was last seen afloat on a
summer's afternoon, July 1545. On that day Henry had assembled
the English Fleet and Army to meet the massed invasion fleet of the
French, who lay anchored off the Isle of Wight. There had already
been some exchange of cannon balls, but nothing more. Henry sat,
fists on hips, on horseback watching the seas before Southsea Castle.

There was silence amongst the ranks, not even a banner flapped,

[*Quoted in Ernle Bradford, *The Story of The Mary Rose*. Hamish Hamilton 1982.]

for there was not a breath of wind. Henry blew, but not even the King of England could command the winds that day. The sound of popping and splintering crashes brought Henry and his aides' attention to the Fleet, sheltering by Horse Sands, from where the noise of mad giggling carried to the shore.

"Oars!" thundered the king.

"Sire, it cannot be helped," said an aide to be helpful; for the French Admiral had sent in small galleys and their oarsmen were manœuvering about, taking pot-shots at the fleet. The sound of French giggles and taunting, and flaunted bare backsides, was too much for Henry. He was as helpless as his Men-of-War, stilled by the calm, while for forty minutes or more the French shredded rigging and lines, they couldn't miss.

The King stared out to sea where the hundreds of French ships waited, outnumbering the English more than two to one. "We must tempt them onto the Spyte,"* mumbled Henry to no-one in particular, for everyone knew the plan. "Then my gunners will find some sport, eh? And my bowmen finish 'em off, close range." Henry was always mindful of wasting ammunition.

"And the sands will feed on Frenchies," said the aide.

"Ay," replied big Henry, "and I'll have thine head, sir, if they do not."

And then it happened. The *Mary Rose* could be seen steering out towards the enemy fleet. "The wind breathes her life," whispered Henry, filling up with pride and joy. He pursed his lips to add his own. "Go my beauty, my *Mary Rose* . . ." and the King of England watched her sail towards the French, then swept his fat fist across the waves.

The King and the entire massed ranks of the English army watched the *Mary Rose*; Henry tilted his head, then tilted it back upright. And the army did the same with much clanking.

"Sire, she's heeling over."

And across the windless air there came the sound of argument, flapping sail, then shrieks. Henry and his army watched in mute horror as the decks of the *Mary Rose* were a mass of tumbling men and armour and weapons. As she listed further they fell into the netting, and then the cannons broke loose and smashed down on top of the lot. The pride of the fleet rolled over and sank beneath the waves without anyone even cursing in the direction of the enemy.

[*'Spyte' now known as the Hamilton Bank.]

On board the French warships and galleys there was silence too. Then a roar of a cheer which carried across the waters and fell upon the ears of dumbstruck Henry. His glazed eyes saw none of the fleshy insults aimed at him from the ships; all he could see were a pair of mastheads sticking out of the waters, and a lone figure waving, frantic and screaming.

"I told thee so . . . I told thee so, knaves."

The French were unable to winkle out Henry's fleet into open engagement on the Solent; they took out their frustration by invading the Isle of Wight for a while, amusing themselves looting and chasing men, women and all manner of animals through the Island before accepting that Henry was not going to come out for annihilation. They sailed for home, and England was safe.

*   *   *

There were a few attempts to bring the *Mary Rose* to the surface at the time, though none succeeded. Then she was forgotten for three hundred years until someone came across her spilled cannon; then forgotten again for another hundred years, when there was the technology to safely submerge the heir to the throne and raise carefully the remains. Charles was the first royal to enter the ship since he who had her built nearly five hundred years before.

The *Mary Rose* was carefully lifted from the water, cradled back to the dockyard and painstakingly reconstructed and treated. Having lain on the sea bed for so long she has lost much of her majesty when compared, say, with the *Victory* next door; she has

A contemporary engraving of the Mary Rose – the only picture of her afloat.

been eaten away, but even the half-carcass is an impressive sight. She rests in a large exhibition hangar, and visitors crowd up onto a raised platform levelled at three-quarters of the way up the ship. Each visitor is given a tape-recorder detailing information about the ship, and as I removed mine from my ear to look at something that caught my eye, there was only the sound of the water which is constantly sprayed onto the wreck. I felt I wanted to be there alone, it was such an experience, and despite the crowds I managed to sidle away and became separated from Wally. As I looked toward the spray and mist that played upon the old timbers I saw two shapes, and knew they were earthbounds, ghosts. I could see a head and a body of each of the two figures, but their legs seemed to trail away into nothing. I had my camera and decided to take a photograph. I took two, then heard a voice close by.

"I crave thine ear to listen to the earthly faults of this villain. I served on the *Mary Rose*, a man in charge of others whose virtues irked me. Saw aught in their good deeds. Minions or varlets ensnared me in a web of hate. Discord led to drink and leaden slumbers, hence I was no longer an honourable man. Became peevish and culled no love among mine fellow men. The discord that surrounded me led me to draw my sword, plucking the life from three wretched men.

As the *Mary Rose* sank to her watery grave methought surely all will be dead men's skulls. Abandoned I became with another villain, then fortune came forth, a light, a woman from mine future. Methinks thou hast commended me to Paradise where I shall surely dwell among angels. Thou madest a picture and by my troth I see'est me, William, traitor to the King by betrayal of trust. Me sayest all this in truth. An abandoned soul is now happy, no more a rebel. 'Tis thus now I thankest thee for sendeth me to a place where I will dwell in peace."

Could William see into the camera and the undeveloped photograph? Often the release of ghosts raises many further questions. For example, had William been down with the rotting timbers all that time, watching the great hulls pass above him in that busy harbour mouth and keeping company with the sealife? Was William condemned to watch sea weed and sludge for over four hundred years; and Jake with him? The ghostly Jake had a strong West-country accent.

"Name be Jake, was the man who had charge of many. Be a

thief, left ship once with others' belongings. Next time drowned, down to the bottom. Fish ate me flesh. I be just bones. Came from a country village, never spied sea 'till joined Man-of-War. I be proud and a thief. Trapped. Brought up from bottom still trapped. Thou hast a good ear, can be free of this water. Got caught up by leg, leg of a thief. Bones found. Thanks be can sail into new waters."

Wally noticed I had taken a photograph and scolded me for wasting a film – nothing would come out of the wreck through all the water and mist. I told him it was my film, and my camera.

"Come along, let's get out of here. It's claustrophobic." He grabbed my arm and pulled me through the crowd. I didn't find it so, yet I do normally suffer from claustrophobia. I wanted to stay, for the *Mary Rose* intrigued me; but then I was hustled along, down the slope and out through a different door where I had to hand back the headset. I couldn't wait to get the film developed.

I expected a picture of the *Mary Rose*, but I didn't really expect a picture of the ghost. The exposures beside it didn't come out at all, only the one with William and Jake, misty marionette-like figures

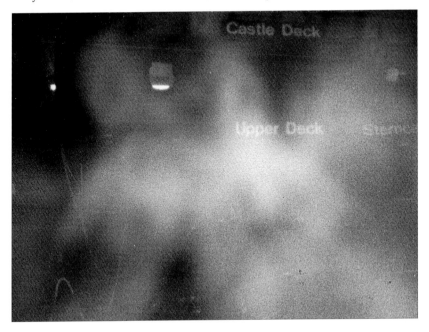

The misty figures of William and Jake on the Mary Rose at Portsmouth.

77

against the dark timbers of the ship. Ghosts can on occasion be captured on film, but don't ask me to explain how.

Some years later I returned to the Dockyard to find a great exhibition hall had been created. The marine archaeologists working on the *Mary Rose* saw the wreck and its well-preserved contents as something of a 'time-capsule' from the Tudor age; for along with the cannon brought to the surface were all manner of other items – pocket sundials, coins, leather clothing, combs, musical instruments, gaming boards and other personal items. When she sank the *Mary Rose* was crowded with 700 men in armour; the fact she was built to carry 400 contributed to the disaster. As I wandered around the tall display cases filled with the contents of the ship, I felt myself being drawn to certain pieces, the bowl of a broken pipe for one.

"Named after the man who should have been King," whispered the ghost beside me. "Arthur, the King's brother, a man of good nature mine sire told me. Thou art a woman who stares at the bowl of the pipe mine sire gave me on one of mine natal days. I am around here, not a prisoner at one place, am free to wander within a short distance; yet free not to ascend to heaven or descend to hell, this am not certain.

Fear is the biggest enemy of man. Take heed of this. Fear of the unknown, fear of not having led a life of perfection. Yet what man walks this path? Fear of drowning, yet drowned was mine fate. This is a day of great cheer. I may continue mine travels to the unknown heaven or hell. Thanks be from the *Mary Rose*, the tomb of so many. Am free, look at mine bowl of pipe, it is special."

It was not long after Arthur had spoken that another presence hovered close and insistent, this time near some old weapons. His voice was deep and strong.

"Weary thou must be, yet I Godfrey, Captain of the Longbowmen, beg thy ear. Release me from hell so may get to the Paradise preacher promised. Mine eyes hast beheld such horror. No torture chamber could hold more. The way down to the ocean bed is not one that entices a man into the embraces of a lustful woman. The cold, the cold, the horror is unspeakable, mine tongue cannot words form. I pushed men overboard so I couldst clutch at the mast; yet even that saveth me not. Am now on the land that was denied mine old age. Mayhap can set forth to redeem mineself in the eyes of the Gods. Farewell."

Indeed the *Mary Rose* was a time-capsule, in more ways than one; though it seems a mind-boggling possibility that ghosts might be condemned to remain underwater with the wreck of their ship. But Jake had said "brought up from waters still trapped", and even bowman Godfrey spoke with relief that he was now "on land". So evidently it is possible to become so earthbound – or rather seabound; then again it's not as if they need air to breathe for their lungs are, technically, dead along with the rest of the body. As already noted, coming across one piece of information in this work can often reveal a further constellation of mysteries.

As for more earthly ones – for centuries historians and marine experts have been mystified over exactly why the *Mary Rose* sank. Some have found answers in faulty design and over-crowding; others reading contemporary accounts note a snatch of conversation between Vice Admiral Carew on board the *Mary Rose* and his uncle Sir Gawain on board the ship which came close by on seeing the flagship heeling over. Just before the fateful moment Sir Gawain called to the *Mary Rose* and asked what was wrong, and the reply came "I have the sort of knaves I cannot rule".

As tradition has it, the captain is supposed to go down with his ship; and so it was. But in one case at least he has come up again – that of the *Mary Rose*. However some 400 years later, Captain Roger Grenville's ghostly comments upon the incident seem only to add to the mystery:

> "Canst thou hearest me? Roger Grenville the captain. Methinks should have insisted there were fewer archers. The captain of the archers were a difficult man. Thy ears are sharp to hearest me, the voice of this soul who hast no body left. Food for the fishes that the good folk of Portsmouth ate. What a feast they hadst.
>
> Have felt guilty. The wrath of the King I couldst feel as I layest on the bed of the sea. See'est I through the tunnel of death a light so this couldst be mine saving from roaming; a spirit without hope. Bless thee good woman, bless thee."

I feel certain that not every victim of the *Mary Rose* disaster was condemned to a watery haunting at the bottom of the sea; nor for that matter the crews and passengers of any other such tragic loss. William and Jake were condemned to their fate – and a particularly horrible one – like so many others because of their misdeeds, and Godfrey for his final unheroic action and possibly others; and

Arthur, assuming he told the whole truth, was trapped through fear of going through the tunnel.

To drown at sea cannot automatically result in a person being denied the passage; consequently I do not believe, for example, that the passengers and the rest of those on the *Titanic* are down below roaming the sea bed of the Atlantic ocean, although one or two might be. As I hope the reader will now be aware, there are only two ways to end up as a ghost – to choose not to go through the passage of light for whatever reason; or to be denied it as punishment.

What kept Captain Grenville down there under the sea is anyone's guess; it is one thing to go down with one's ship, but quite another to remain with it for ever after.

CHAPTER NINE

H.M.S. VICTORY

G ATHERED TOGETHER on the quayside by the *Victory*, awaiting
their tour guide, were several parties of French school-
children and their teachers. I have sometimes wondered
what the ghosts on board thought of these times when the children
come visiting the shrine of the fallen hero who led the *Victory* against
the ships of their forefathers. There seemed no malice upon the
children's faces, only varieties of boredom, curiosity and excitement.

By the time of the Battle of Trafalgar, the English Navy had
solved the problem which had helped cause the *Mary Rose* to go
under – the problem of gunports and waterline; it had ironed out the
potential for disagreement among crew members which had bedevilled the *Mary Rose*'s tragic manœuvring that summer day. The
Victory, like other ships of the line, was superior in discipline,
gunnery and battle seamanship, and that was why in the autumn of
1805 it was the English Fleet which stalked the enemy sheltering in
the harbour of Cadiz. Nelson wanted them to come out and fight.
And fight they did.

There is little evidence of the ravages of the great sea battle which
made the *Victory* so famous, when she had led the attack and braved
the fire-storm of the enemy ships off the coast of Trafalgar. The holes
have been plugged, timbers replaced, as were the masts and rigging;
in fact only the lower decks remain of the original ship. In her
restoration she is a majestic vision, in her warpaint of black and gold
and bristling with guns. The French children were led inside by a
guide who spoke their language, and some few minutes later we
followed with our own.

The tour guide, an elderly bespectacled man in Naval uniform,
gathered his flock of visitors before him and led us up the gangplank
and into the ship. He smiled and waited patiently while all finished
their last-minute fidget, then introduced himself and touched his
hat. He then slapped a low beam, "Watch yer 'eads, and yer step,
ladies and gentlemen," said he, next pointing down to the lines of
polished cannonballs. "Welcome to the *Victory*."

Despite its huge size from the outside, the interior of the *Victory*
is warren-like and dark; the ship's timbers crowd low and threat-
ening, the stepways steep and dangerous. Every few feet stand the

huge cannon and arranged around them on the floors more lines of cannonballs. In the spaces between, above and around are the instruments for feeding and firing the now cold beasts of war. One tourist banged his head as he climbed a stairway, while another slipped on a cannonball. The guide cast a wary look at each as he waited at the top, then when the last of the visitors reached the summit, he bent his knees and welcomed us to the Captain's Cabin.

The cabin is the only place, apart from the deck, with a feel of light and space, for the entire rear wall is window. The cabin is comfortable and spacious and offers lovely views. Arranged around the cabin are tasteful pieces of period furniture, chairs and a desk, and I sensed there was a presence. I felt it come close beside me, as if it too was watching the guide demonstrating the incredible fighting efficiency of the fighting ship, for everything was on hinges and could be raised for battle.

"Of course, the furniture was carried in a boat behind," explained the guide, "and enemy captains would not fire on these."

I thought I felt the presence shift slightly, the air seemed to shiver. If it was a ghost, there was no time to let it speak as the guide was pressing on, again with the reminder to "Watch yer 'eads". The troupe were led down some steps and out onto the deck, where it

H.M.S. Victory.

was delicious to breathe again fresh air after the polish fumes and mustiness down below. The stragglers caught up and joined the semi-circle in front of the guide, and all followed his finger to the small brass plaque laid into the timbers of the decking. The guide cleared his throat and everyone fell silent.

"Ladies and gentlemen, today it is quiet; but try and imagine you're in the midst of battle. There is smoke and fire, there are screams and explosions . . ." and I tried to imagine cannonballs crashing through the rigging and the deck awash with blood and water, and of course the deafening boom-boom of the cannon down below. The guide assumed an action stance. "Nelson headed straight for the enemy fleet, every sail the masts could bear, for there wasn't much wind that day. He pierced the enemy's line and then went looking for Admiral Villeneuve, who led the Combined Fleet of France and Spain."

The guide looked around at each visitor in turn, his eyes wide. "It was a storm of fire but Nelson calm as you please paced the Quarter Deck in full honours. Then . . ." and he waited while the image of Nelson was in the mind of all, "then the *Victory* came by the stern of the *Bucentaure,* opened fire and sent a broadside into the heart of Admiral Villeneuve's flagship."

His voice took on a different tone as he raised his pointed finger upwards. "See up there?" and everyone looked. "That's called a Fighting Top." It was a high platform fixed around the masts. "Well, on the other side of the *Victory* was the *Redoubtable,* and she crashed into the bow and the two ships were locked together, side by side."

The Navy-man traced his finger from the Fighting Top downwards to the brass plaque on the deck. "From up there a musket-man on the *Redoubtable* had a clear shot at Nelson and fired. The bullet fizzed and took the Admiral in the left chest, then ricocheted down his spine."

There was silence. The guide gathered himself while all peered at the brass plaque. "There Nelson fell." Again there was silence.

"If you'll follow me, ladies and gentlemen, I will take you down below. Mind yer 'eads," and he was sliding down into the bowels of the ship. I could feel the ghostly presence hovering, I knew it wanted to speak; there was no opportunity for I too had to follow the guide, but I felt the ghost come along, always close, but not heavy like some ghosts. The presence felt gentle.

Deeper and deeper we travelled, on each deck the headspace was lower, and the stepways steeper. On the lower gundeck it was dark and cramped and the smell was not so much of polish, though that was there in plenty; it was another atmosphere, altogether different, something old. The visitors crouched low as they stumbled through the cannon-filled realm of shadow and lantern-light, and emerged in a small cramped space to find the guide waiting, hat in hand beside a large barrel. Next to it, illuminated with soft light, stood an easel with an oil painting framed with gold.

The picture showed a nearby rib of the ship against which the dying Nelson was laid. The guide said nothing, and all took the opportunity of marking the silence too. At last he spoke. "It was here they brought the wounded Admiral . . ." and he began to give an account of the last few hours of the hero's life.

Exactly what he said I could not hear, for there was a ghost shouting so loudly for my attention I barely had time to find my pencil and paper.

"I be press-ganged. Name is John. I was here on this deck running for the surgeon. 'Bring this, bring that!' A bad-tempered man. I be very angry when the Admiral was killed, all me fault I thought. Tripped over a body on the way here and broke me wrist, so was no good running for more salt and more brandy that the surgeon kept calling for. Me wrist was hanging awkward.

Cannot speak much, have been scared to go on. I got killed in a battle afterwards, have been here ever since. So many people stare yet never see me. Would the Admiral have lived if I could have fetched what I was sent for? Blamed meself. Surgeon angry with me. You can hear me, thank God for that. I shall learn much when I get to the light. My thanks to you for hearing."

Knowing the extent of the damage done by the musketball, it is unlikely poor John could have prevented the death of Nelson; but then he was not to know that at the time. He had waited, amongst the last of the crew to leave the *Victory*; perhaps a fitting testimony to how much Nelson was loved by those who served him.

And those who have followed, for as John concluded his confession I heard the tour guide explaining how on special occasions the senior officers in the Royal Navy gather in that strange dark corner of the *Victory* to pay homage. Who knows if any of them, as they too stood, hats off and heads bowed in contemplation, have sensed the ghostly presence who undoubtedly joins them on each such solemn occasion?

"I have followed you madam. I pray you may heed this soul, so well known yet so unworthy of the attention given. I am Thomas Hardy, the man who held Nelson as he died. I fear I may be responsible for this great man's death. At that time had persuaded him on deck in the height of battle. He had retreated to his cabin to get something, I know not what. I called him to hurry, he did so, and fell. Had he been a moment later he would have escaped this terrible injury that caused him to depart at that time to the next world.

This incident haunted me for the rest of my life. I fear laughter was never heard coming from my mouth. Having been a prisoner in that place where he died, have learnt much. There are mighty ones who decree when a man should die, so my guilt has been in vain; yet could not leave. You madam send me on a voyage unknown, but welcome. Thank you."

Thomas Masterman Hardy, the famous flag captain of the *Victory*, who went on to become First Sea Lord in 1830 before death in 1839. His final testimony seems to create even more controversy than the old famous one of Nelson's last request.* There was no time to ask him, there was no time to think, for the guide was pressing on, ushering the visitors back through the dark deck of the ship.

As I ducked and clambered I felt something tugging at my shoulder, insistent. There was nothing for it but to stop and listen to a ghost with a rather different attitude to kissing a fellow sailor.

"I too have been waiting my turn to speak. A common seaman who loved the taste of salt on his lips, who was happier at sea than being a land lubber, yet was not a kindly man. Had a passion for the young lads aboard. Clapped in irons once when caught, cat-o'-nine tails another time; but boys, oh yes boys, loved 'em. Now may sail on as see a light. No more boys no more. Am off to be a landlubber in heaven I hopes."

The tour guide was watching me as I finished writing what the ghost had said. He seemed a little impatient, but how could I explain what had been taking place? "If you would come this way, madam, we shall find our way out." He slapped a low beam and grinned, and I took the warning as he turned and I followed him around and down, and up and through and finally out of a hole in the side where the rest of the party stepped carefully down a gangplank to the ground on the other side of the ship.

[*Either Nelson said "'Tis Kismet, Hardy" or, more likely, "Kiss me, Hardy". Naval historians conclude it was the latter.

The tour was over, but something was still with me and although quite weary from the contortions and concentration I was pleased to find time for the ghost of Gladys Parsons:

"How many years have I waited, 60, 65? I do not know. Lost count. Came here with my husband and three-year-old son to look over the *Victory*. They had warned us the ceilings were low and to mind your head. The little one was tired and I picked him up and carried him. We went down some steps, at the bottom I ducked to avoid striking my head but failed to lower my son, consequently he banged his head.

Of course everyone fussed around him and a bump soon came up. We left the ship and bought him an ice cream to stop him crying. He developed a bit of a fever but was over it in a couple of days but to my horror he never spoke again. The blow on his head had affected his brain. He became nearly an imbecile, all because of my carelessness. I never forgave myself. My husband went off with another woman two years later, leaving me with an idiotic son. I have haunted down here in this old ship all these years believing myself wicked. You show me the way out. I am so grateful. My name is Gladys Parsons and my son was called David."

*   *   *

Many of my Christian friends say that what I do is wicked, that these spirits are really evil demons and part of Satan's dark army. I guess Mrs Parsons and all the other earthbounds would find it a seriously depressing experience to be confronted by a determined priest declaring them evil spirits and casting them down to hell and damnation.

CHAPTER TEN

H.M.S. WARRIOR

OUTSIDE THE dockyard waits the *Warrior*, a once fearsome beast of the seas, the pride of Queen Victoria's Navy, launched in the 1860s to scare the French. She is big and black and made of iron, and in her day packed the very latest hi-tech weapons, with pivot guns, shells and cannonballs, a propeller for when the wind was still, and a hide thicker than a rhino's.

Nearly fifty years after the defeat of Napoleon at Waterloo, the French had launched the world's first ironclad steam warship and England again feared invasion; for should the French come to Portsmouth as they had in 1545 with such a fleet, England's Navy would be blown from the waters. The Navy responded with iron ships of its own, the *Warrior* for one.

Over four hundred feet long, the heart of the *Warrior* is an armoured "citadel" whose walls are four and a half inch iron backed by eighteen inches of prime teak, then another inch or so of more iron; all fixed to an iron framework. And inside this is another thick skin of pine. The *Warrior* cost a fortune to build, but she was the most formidable battleship the world had ever seen. And the ship's cook was just as tough.

> "Listen to me carefully lady. I was the cook on the *Warrior*," hissed the ghost. "It was a hard job trying to cook for so many men with only a young lad as my assistant. I was often burnt on the stove in rough seas. The lad on one particular voyage was hopeless; we had been engaged in a battle and food had to be cooked. The lad got burnt falling on the stove. I was furious and beat him unmercifully. He died of his burns they said, but my beating did not help. I blamed myself, should have had sympathy, but that was not my nature. A hard man to know and harder to work for. I have remained on the ship since my death. Some men working on it have seen me. I was a very bad man. Can go on to rest I hope, am so very tired. Thank you for releasing me. I never want to cook again if I am coming back to live again."

The *Warrior*, although over 150 years old, remains a fearsome-looking warship to the landlubber who visits the historic dockyard;

and perhaps might still prove so to any rubber-crafted invasion of England, should such an attack ever fall upon Portsmouth.

H.M.S. Warrior.

CHAPTER ELEVEN

CARISBROOKE CASTLE

IN SPRINGTIME when the yellow primroses push through the green surrounding the old castle at Carisbrooke, it is a picture. Its grey stone crumbles here and there, and some of the battlements have broken, but the walls are largely intact. Carisbrooke Castle will forever be remembered as the prison of King Charles I, though without doubt the history of the site dates back beyond recorded time when on this Island lived a peoples with a whole different outlook on heaven and earth, even when it rained. But chances are like the rest of us they too enjoyed the spring and summer days, and the cool shade of its leafy trees.

Sadly, Charles was not so lucky. There are many accounts of the king's incarceration, and most report his stay was during the wettest year anyone could remember; some say it rained from May Day until September with scarce three dry days together. Who knows what is the perfect weather for a breakout, but rain and rain and rain, and mud, must add complications to delicate plans.

The King of England fretted at the thought of assassins who he believed were coming to get him at Hampton Court Palace, where Cromwell had placed him since his defeat in the English Civil War. The idea of escape came in a flash during a firework display on the 5th November 1647. Now the king aimed to scoot, but how, and where? He asked his former servants Colonel John Ashburnham and Sir John Berkeley to come up with a good plan.

And so on a stormy wet November night King Charles I placed a note on the table explaining he was retiring himself from public view, then stepped quietly down a back staircase, opened the door and fled ... Within hours the king was lost in the forests. He, his Groom of the Bedchamber and the two Johns found themselves at a cross of paths and a big old tree.

"Which way?"

The King of England chewed his lip.

"Majesty, we must hurry, already the alarm will be raised ..." Then, "Look." And the group stared at what looked like torches in the sky. Charles mopped several droplets of water from the end of his nose. "'Tis Windsor castle ..."

"Allow me, Majesty," enquired the Groom of the Bedchamber,

but the king brushed away the offered handkerchief. "This way!" and crashed on down the path.

By the dawn light the rains had eased somewhat and the king was confident. He had found the rendez-vous for fresh horses and had put some serious mileage between his party and any pursuers.

"I cannot think clearly in the saddle," announced Charles at last. "Come, sirs, let us walk our beasts and consider our plans."

And so the four dismounted and led their horses through the wet meadows of Hampshire. The King of England gazed up into the grey cloud-filled skies. "Colonel. Tell me again of your cunning plan and the Isle of Wight."

Colonel Ashburnham offered a withering look to Sir John Berkeley, then spoke. "Your Majesty must remain in the country to rally support. Who knows what opportunities might arise with Parliament and even the Scots. All is not lost, Majesty. As they say, it is not over until the fat friar squeals."

"Sir John?" queried the king.

"Your Majesty must find a boat. Jersey is ..."

The colonel cut him short. "Your Majesty is acquainted with the Isle of Wight. There are many there loyal to our cause."

"Not enough," grumbled Charles. "It is pleasant, I admit – but not such good potatoes."

"Jersey would be better by far," fretted the noble Sir John, and tugged his horse forward, closer to the king. "Find a boat, Majesty, or at least head for the West Country."

"Majesty," interrupted the colonel, and he too trotted forward, almost level with Charles. "There are signs the new Governor of the Island will be helpful."

"He is an Army man!" spat Sir John.

"He is no extremist, as His Majesty well suspects. Far from it. I feel sure he will deter any would-be assassin."

The two Johns were trotting fast to keep pace with the king. "And besides," continued the colonel, "the Island is still England; and close enough to monitor developments in Parliament, and should your Majesty wish, you can negotiate with the Army via the Governor."

"Legge?" asked the king of his groom.

"Majesty?"

"What have you to offer on the matter?"

The groom rushed forward, handkerchief in hand.

"Tssk," said the King of England, wiping his nose.

"Your Majesty cannot be better placed," continued the colonel. "Portsmouth is next door and should defections occur in the Navy they might rally in an instant."

Sir John opened his mouth to make another attempt to check the cunning plan before His Majesty was hooked. In his mind the words "Get a boat, tonight, tomorrow at the latest" were on their way to his mouth but the colonel was there before him. "Your Majesty has friends on the Island, the good knight Sir John."

The king fingered a sodden curl.

"And anyway," concluded the colonel icily towards Sir John Ashburnham, "if the King of England fled the country the Scots would be angry, and the world would laugh."

"Let them." Sir John was almost shaking with rage and cold at the colonel's cooing. "At least you will be safe. Majesty, get a boat, I say."

The colonel sighed. "Of course, if all else fails, being so close to the sea, it being an island and all, your Majesty will find little difficulty finding a boat, or even a dozen, to make good your escape."

King Charles stopped suddenly and sniffed the air. "Can you smell that, sirs?"

The two Johns wrinkled their noses, while Legge was ready with his cloth.

"The sea." The king turned to his companions. "Legge and I shall wait with the Earl of Southampton while you, Sir John, and the colonel go over to the Island and sound out this Governor."

It is recorded that Governor Robert Hammond was on his way to a meeting when the two Johns found him; the colonel opened the conversation by blurting the news of the king's escape and the threats to his life; and according to those reports Governor Hammond turned pale and nearly fell off his horse in amazement to learn the king was so close and required his protection. The Governor is remembered as saying: "Oh gentlemen, you have undone me by bringing the king to the Island. If at least you have brought him; and if you have not, pray let him not come; for what between my duty to His Majesty, and my gratitude for this fresh obligation of confidence, and my observing my trust to the Army, I shall be confounded."

The colonel stared at the Governor and a good few moments passed before he spoke. "No matter, no harm done if you do not receive the king," and pulled his horse around.

"But then again . . ." called Governor Hammond, "if something happened to the king, the Army and the Kingdom would hold me responsible for not giving aid." He shifted in his saddle and cast an eye over the soldiers with him, then turned to the colonel and Sir John. "Since the king has come all this way to save his life and chooses me to protect him, I will do all that is expected from a person of honour or honesty."

There was silence between the men, only the sound of the horses' snorting interrupted the delicate situation. Finally it was Sir John Berkeley who spoke. "That is not enough of a guarantee."

The Governor silenced the protest with a wave of his mit. "That is for the king to decide. Let's go see him now."

"With all my heart!" trumpeted the colonel.

Sir John was stunned, and hissed a whisper at the colonel: "Do you mean to carry this man to the king before you know whether he will approve? Undoubtedly you will surprise him."

The Governor was calling to his men. "We shall pick up Captain Basket from Cowes Castle along the way." He turned to Sir John.

"Perhaps you, sir, should wait for us here."

King Charles I and Colonel Hammond, Governor of Carisbrooke Castle.

Sir John Berkeley gazed upon the gates of Carisbrooke Castle and shuddered.

When the colonel found him, the king was edgy and nervous, pacing the room and chewing his nails. On sight of the colonel, Charles looked resolved. "We have considered Sir John's idea of a boat, and it is a good one. Why just this past hour I have . . ."

"Your Majesty," interrupted the colonel, "I have with me Governor Hammond and Basket down below."

The king's jaw dropped and quivered for a full minute while his eyeballs spun around in their sockets, round and round and at last coming to a stop in the middle, and both then focused upon the colonel. "You've done what!"

Charles was busy searching the colonel's face for sign of tease, but there was none. "Oh you have undone me, for I am by this means made fast from stirring."

The colonel, seeing the disappointment on his sovereign's face, offered to go downstairs and deal with the soldiers while the king escaped, but Charles was already shaking his head and gazing into a point of space far above and beyond the colonel's head. "I understand you well enough, but the world would not excuse me," said

Carisbrooke Castle and Gatehouse.

he. "If I should follow this counsel it will be said and believed that you ventured your life for me, and that I had unworthily taken it from you. No," sighed the King of England, "it is too late now for thinking of anything but going through the way you have forced me upon, and leave the issue to God."

And thus King Charles I became a guest of the great castle at Carisbrooke.

*   *   *

The castle entrance is narrow and dark, and as the visitor draws closer the arrangement of the gatehouse brings on the feeling of stepping into the mouth of a monster; the stone on either side is rounded like fat jowls and above the opening are two tiny windows, like eyes. Through the entrance the stone is scarred and pock-marked and it is twenty paces or so upwards to the old wooden gate, then the visitor steps inside Carisbrooke Castle.

Behind the gatehouse can be found steps leading up to the battlements, and halfway up is a doorway to a ruined room with crumbling walls and a ceiling open to the rain. There is a sign reading Armoury, and one day I found myself in that room, staring at an old fireplace which had barely escaped the ravages of ruin.

Interior of the Gatehouse Armoury.

I walked about five paces into the room with my friend Sue Robertson following close behind, when I noticed the fireplace was alive with a lovely log fire. I looked around and instead of cold broken stone, the windows were covered with beautiful blue curtains, a deep Royal blue; there was carpet on the floor and a table at which two men were sat facing each other and deep in discussion. They sat side by side, not facing across the table, and each wore a black curled wig. I stared in total amazement at the pair, but they seemed not to notice either of us.

The pair at the table wore knee breeches and stockings; one in a plain brown jacket, the other wore a more decorative blue coat. The man in plain brown sat with his legs crossed in a manly, extravagant way, and resting his elbow on his knee. I looked at Sue and she was staring at me with wide eyes. "Can you see anything?" she asked in whisper.

"Yes," I said, equally softly so as not to disturb the two men in their conversation.

"We're back in the past," said Sue excitedly.

"Don't tell me," I pleaded, "don't tell me a thing you see yet, as no-one will ever believe us. Let's get out of here." But neither of us moved, for the two figures and the warm fire and the curtains were so real I could have sat down with them, or brushed the dust from a shoulder.

As we backed out through the doorway, at last, the scene began to fade; the damp drizzle ran down the cold stone walls, the blue curtains were gone, the carpet too; and the fireplace was cold and dead. We both kept silent. Inside the gatehouse a room has been turned into an exhibition with photographs and sketches of the castle's famous inhabitants and visitors. I gave Sue a piece of paper and a pencil and told her to write down everything she had seen in that ruined room.

We sat on the exhibition room floor, at opposite ends, and each of us made lists: the fire, the blue curtains, how the men sat at the table. There was no doubt Sue had seen exactly what I had, it all checked. Then a picture on the wall caught my eye, and Sue's, for we both stood and looked. "That's the man, the man sitting with his legs crossed," said Sue. Indeed it was, though the picture portrayed him wearing a different coat; but it was the same face for certain.

The flight of King Charles and his subsequent imprisonment in Carisbrooke Castle has puzzled historians for centuries – did he jump or was he pushed, ever so sweetly-reasoned towards his doom? Some see it as an odd coincidence that Hammond just happened to be Governor at that time. He was one of Cromwell's favoured young officers and at twenty-seven years of age he had influence in Army Committees; and through a seemingly bizarre and miraculous coincidence of fate, Parliament so happened to hurry through his appointment as Captain and Governor of the Island. It is said, on hearing the news of the king's arrival at Carisbrooke, dour Oliver Cromwell was especially happy and even broke a smile amongst his fellow officers at Army HQ.

London newsletters reporting on the incident of Charles' escape to the castle noted with interest the remarkable coincidence of the king's arrival just after Hammond as nothing less than a mystical revelation on the new Governor's part. Indeed they were strange days, even for the king whose first night on the Island was spent at the Plume of Feathers inn, and there engraved on his bedstead were the words "Remember Thy End". King Charles ran his gloved fingers across the words, then fell to his knees and prayed for three solid hours; and upon hearing the news as he knelt to pray in Saint Mary's church in Brading, the good knight Sir John Oglander found tears in his eyes.

Other commentators, however, have noted the strange coincidence that Governor Hammond's uncle was one of the king's own chaplains; and only days before Charles' departure from Hampton Court, Hammond had been brought before the king and kissed the royal hand.

Soon after Charles' arrival at the castle the Governor told the nobles of the Island about the unexpected visitation and informed them he had tightened security on the ferries and ports; then invited them to come see the king.

"Desioring to bee somewhat secure till soom happye accommodacion maye be mayde betweene mee and my P'rliament," said his Majesty to the bemused bunch of nobles gathered before him, "I have putt myselve in this place; for I desior not a drop moore of Christian bloude showlde bee spilt, neythor doo I desior to bee chargeable to anye of you; I shall not desior soe mutch as a capon from anye of you."*

While Cromwell moved his Army headquarters into Windsor Castle, the king planned his comeback. There was much work to be done, for the thorny issues of politics and religion had bedevilled his

[*Quoted in *The Royal Prisoner.* Jack D. Jones. Lutterworth Press 1965.]

kingdom. The Governor ignored orders for the arrest of the two Johns and accepted the king's assurances that he would not try to escape from Carisbrooke. Sir John Berkeley was still arguing for a boat, everyone knew that, but everyone ignored him; even the king who busied himself writing *aides memoirs* and treaties to anyone he could think of who might help.

For exercise he walked with the Governor, or went hunting in the nearby forests. Meanwhile the Governor daily received orders from Parliament and the Army to watch all visitors and drum up some extra guards, on which he thought deeply. And so too did Charles. "I am daily more and more satisfied with this Governor," noted His Majesty King Charles I. To keep the king happy Parliament sent over his favourite furniture and servants to remind him of home; they even arranged for the royal coach to be shipped across so as he could tour the Island in style.

But at Army HQ there were rumours that the queen was seen in Jersey buying up barrels of wine and cartloads of nice cheeses for a party, and again the Governor was ordered to increase security around the king. There was also an order, for the king's own protection of course, to lock Charles' room at night. The Governor accepted the king's word that he had always intended to come to Carisbrooke and nowhere else, but he still locked the door as ordered.

There were plenty of visitors during the day, and during Christmas time a Committee of Parliamentary Commissioners came from London to put their terms to the king, terms for Parliament to take control of the armed forces and in time the abolition of all bishops and heaven knew what else.

The day after, Christmas Day, there arrived a party of Scottish Commissioners to talk with Charles; and when the doors were closed and the Governor out of earshot, the king spoke quietly: "I have a cunning plan,"said he. "Raise an army in Scotland and come rescue me and restore me to the throne."

The old Scot studied the royal countenance and noted the uneven way the king's wig had shifted off-balance. "We shall expect something in return," he said at last. "Changes to land rights and the correct worship of God."

"Of course, anything, you'll see," whispered the King of England.

The old Scot came close to the royal ear. "Can we have that in writing?"

And so the deal was made, copied and placed in a lead box, then buried in a garden so as no Englishman might find it.

The English Commissioners were not best pleased with Charles when they returned for his reply to their proposals; it was clear he was up to something, and to add insult to injury he bid the Governor take them out of his presence. As they filed out of the meeting room the Governor noted the stormy expressions and remembered the Scots on Christmas Day, who despite their downcast gazes several had been smiling, and one fool as he left was positively skipping along whistling some French ditty. The Governor felt the throbbing in his temples and the pain in between, and wondered on a good cure for a headache. Charles was ready to escape.

The interior of Carisbrooke Castle has altered somewhat since Charles' day. Some of the original buildings remain, but over the years repairs and rebuilding have taken place. As for the outside, below the castle walls 300 years' worth of rubbish has sedimented and thus a leap over the walls is not such a long drop. Not that Charles intended to go over the top at first, but out through the open gate.

The king packed away his small things, pulled on his boots and coat. The queen had been told to ready a boat and while the Scots army gathered he would be enjoying Jersey's lovely potatoes. All was set, and the chance came; Governor Hammond was out of the castle. Even the wind was right. Charles took a last look around the castle, spat and just to be sure took another look at the weather vane. The vane! It had changed completely. Charles heard shouts by the gatehouse – it was the Governor, ordering the gates be closed and the guard be doubled.

The king was no longer guest, but prisoner.

*   *   *

The tales of hauntings at Carisbrooke Castle are numerous; all manner of wraiths and mysterious happenings have been reported over the years, and one look at the old castle when the mists enshroud its battlements is enough to make even the sceptical shudder and wonder. I did not have to wait long before a ghost spoke, though already in the armoury room behind the gatehouse I had heard a whisper; but as Sue and I descended the steps I noticed a shadowy figure just inside the gatehouse archway. The figure was dwarfed by the massive old wooden gates. Sue did not see him, but guessed there was something around and so waited quietly while I wrote down his words. His voice was thin and desperate:

"Thy attention if thou pleaseth. I pray for release for this wicked villain. The king wished for water in his closet, yet I took it not, therefore he remaineth dirty and washed not. I did not serve his meals at the correct hour. Oh if thou could understand the thoughts of this soul who was of noble birth yet had to wait upon the king; who is now trapped having committed many cruel deeds towards a man who was innocent apart from his majestic birth.

I have suffered by getting no further than these gates. A prison not only for the king but for his attendant as well. Henry is the name I was given. A tunnel opens and my journey is to begin; may it have a joyful ending. Accept my gratitude for thy attention. Thou hast helped me onwards."

It is impossible to confirm the identity of this ghost, for the king's servants and staff were numerous and without a surname it is mere guesswork as to which Henry of several it might have been; but the fact of his negligence suggests he must have been amongst the new staffing arrangements ordered by Parliament, for Parliament and Cromwell were not happy with Charles. Nor for that matter was Governor Hammond; he wrote to his seniors requesting that either the king be removed or he be discharged from his duty. The request was denied.

There are many accounts of Charles I's imprisonment at Carisbrooke Castle during that abysmally wet year. Were William Shakespeare alive after the event no doubt there would have been a play, and who knows whether it would have been tragedy or comedy; though the end result proved a disaster for all concerned. From Christmas 1647 onwards and into the New Year Carisbrooke was busy with suspicion and plot. The two Johns found themselves dismissed and the Governor introduced the king to some new companions to attend him two by two, and who were to sleep touching his door at night. But it was well known Sir John and the Colonel had opted for Plan B and waited on the mainland shore with a boat and fingers to the wind.

Although there were orders to prevent letters coming and going between the king and those outside, it was a difficult business to suppress. The Governor suspected everyone of plotting to get the king out; though the Royalists too were suspicious as somehow for every cunning plan hatched, it found an equally canny report being delivered by the Parliamentary spy network, and thus the Governor was wise to boats and strangers in the area. There were plans discovered to break the king out through his ceiling, but this was soon discounted for Charles believed he could squeeze through the bars of his window. He had tested the gap with his head and was confident of following with the rest of the royal personage.

The night set for escape was a wet one. Outside the castle walls waited Edward Worsley, son of Gatcombe House, with a clean pair of gloves and boots. All knew the plan; the king would squeeze through the bars, climb down the rope provided by Henry Firebrace, his servant, then lower himself over the battlements and scoot. The horses were ready and so was a boat. Firebrace waited beneath the window and from the gatehouse came the sound of "haw haw haw". The guards were drunk and getting drunker. It was perfect.

"Majesty," whispered Firebrace through the wet air as he stood below the window, shaking the rope, "all is well, all is ready. Come now!"

But all he could hear were grunts and oofs. "Majesty!" he called again.

But all he could hear was the same, and getting weaker. "Majesty!"

"What!" hissed the King of England from above.

"What keeps you, Majesty?"

The king made another gasp. "I'm stuck, Firebrace. Me eeeeers are through but not the rest."

Then silence. Then a curse. "Damme..."

And the second Civil War erupted.

*　　*　　*

I could not stop thinking about the room in the gatehouse and the timeslip Sue and I had experienced. What had the two men been discussing? They did not seem antagonistic, more friendly, conspiratorial almost. It was soon after the ghostly Henry that another ghost spoke. He had been roaming the battlements, though since he belongs to another part of Carisbrooke's long history I shall tell you of him another time. On that day I was keen to discover the secret of the room and the two figures we had seen.

It is hard to equate the man we saw with descriptions of the king after the abortive window escape. It is said he stopped filing his nails and cutting his hair and beard, and even the Governor's fine new bowling green cheered him only a little. King Charles contented himself on wet days praying and reading psalms and sermons or the Bible. When these tired him he quilled a poem of his own and called it "Majesty in Misery"; and a wholesome chapter for his new novel, entitled "Contemplations on Death".

The Governor did his best to dispel such gloom by playing bowls on the new green, and by all accounts it did brighten His Majesty who made sport with witticisms to amuse the players and attendants; though calling the Scots cowards did raise an eyebrow or two. Even the good Sir John Oglander came up for a game when the weather permitted.

I guess you can keep a good man in, but you can't keep him down. Charles pondered on the problem of the iron bars. "Some instrument must be had to remove the bar," wrote His Majesty in secret code. "I think it is called the endless Screw or the grat Force."

Unable to find such machines, Firebrace instead arranged for a good assortment of files to be smuggled into the castle, plus some saws and acid for good measure. Meanwhile the Governor pondered on the very same thing through the reports sent to him. Firebrace also suggested the king might try dressing up in a false beard, wig, coloured drawers, big shoes and a broad hat and float out with the masses who came to see the king to be healed.* But again the Governor was alert to the plan. It was clear to the Royalists that someone, somewhere within the network of support was betraying Charles and the efforts to get him away.

In the spring of 1648 Charles was found new rooms next to the officers' quarters and the determined Firebrace proposed a new plan. A backstairs window was ideal for a breakout for the drop to the ground was less; but there were sentries outside. If only they could be bribed to look the other way, then . . . it just might be possible. The king studied the guard rosters and eyed the soldiers carefully, then decided on a likely trio. They were offered £100 apiece and assured of forgiveness for past allegiances if only they would close their eyes at the right moment. The three agreed and the plan was set.

In his quarters the Governor opened the latest dispatch from London: "Four horses lie in or near Portsmouth to carry the King . . . A Parliament man who liveth near Arundell is the likely guide. The man is supposed to be Sir Edward Alford . . . the place by

[*Known as the 'King's Evil'. Touching royalty was thought to cure scrofula or tuberculosis.]

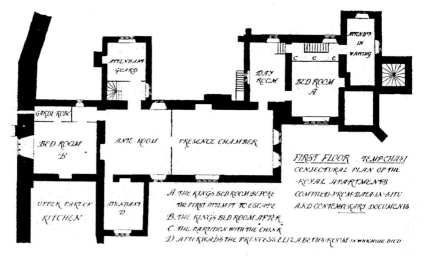

Layout of the first floor rooms.

which the King is to escape is a low room through a window, or a window that is but slightly made up."

The Governor unwrapped the next dispatch and read how the proposed escape was still on, that a ship was ready, and to be vigilant that week-end of May 28th.

As midnight approached on Sunday 28th, Charles checked his acid and tucked away a pair of grey stockings. He wobbled the bars and they shifted like milk teeth. Outside the castle walls waited Edward Worsley, again with horse ready, and Charles thought of the boat beyond to carry him to freedom. The King of England poked his head between the broken bars and out of the window.

And the Scots crossed the border into England to join the Royalist uprising.

* * *

There is puzzlement to this day as to how the King's moves were so well anticipated, and some historians have suggested possible culprits.* Yet even though the guards that night saw fit to blow the whistle a half hour before midnight and the Governor had men ready, in truth Robert Hammond already had warning of a window. I am sure one ghost of Carisbrooke Castle knew more than he let on to me, despite confessing his betrayal . . .

[*The Rev. Boucher James points the finger at a man named Lilly. See his *Letters Archæological and Historical Relating to the Isle of Wight*.]

"A feeling of guilt is a sorrowful possession. 'Twas me, a man with a sense of duty, who reported the King was endeavouring to escape through a window. I was not a guard; thought His Majesty was a man to admire, yet had to keep these thoughts deep within mineself. Why didst I not allow him to escape? He was taken away across the Solent and beheaded. Mine guilt weighed heavily upon me. Mayhap he would have been caught away from here, yet mayhap he would have got away.

Each day I awoke with a heavy heart. Could not leave this cursed place when mine life ended, remained a spirit. Rest was denied me. My name is Edward who was praised for this act of betrayal. Am I forgiven? As can see a light which draws me away. Shall not resist it, but leave here feeling happier than I have ever been."

I do not think this is the ghost of Edward Worsley any more than Henry is Firebrace. Neither gave surnames so it is impossible to identify them for certain, so who knows who they were? The mystery must remain for now.

The news of Cromwell's victory over the Scots and the crushing of the Royalist uprising was told the king during a game of bowls. The sound of clacking wood scarcely masked the noise of Charles' grinding teeth. He eyed the bowl at his feet and thought of kicking it hard. Governor Robert Hammond took up the jack and rolled it across the green to the far side.

"It is the worst news that ever came to England," fumed the king. The Governor watched the little ball come to a rest. "If Cromwell had lost, the Scots would have the thrones of England *and* Scotland." King Charles held the bowl in his hand and rounded on Hammond. "You are mistaken. I could have commanded them back with the motion of my hand," and with that he launched the bowl towards the target . . .

*　　*　　*

"The most mysterious and melancholy incident in the tragedy of the eight months captivity of Charles I in Carisbrooke Castle," laments the Reverend James,* once vicar of Saint Mary's church in Carisbrooke, is that of the Prince of Wales and the Queen, Henrietta Maria. For the prince sailed for England with a fleet and joined the ships of the Navy which had declared for the king during the

[*Rev. E. Boucher James, *Letters Archæological and Historical.*]

uprising. The Island, and Carisbrooke Castle at that moment, suggests the good vicar, was vulnerable and the king quite rescuable; and nothing else could have saved his life. The prince faced the ships which had not defected and ordered them to strike their flag. They would not. The Prince of Wales eyed their defiance then set sail for London. There he demanded support. London refused. He asked the City for £20,000. This too was refused, and when the Navy gathered more ships against him he sailed away to the Continent and the strange delights of the Netherlands without even attempting to rescue his father.

Meanwhile, the queen preferred not to speak of the matter; some say no-one wanted Charles in France, and anyway Henrietta Maria was already preparing to marry another.

There is another mysterious and melancholy incident concerning the fate of King Charles. In the castle on Windsor Hill, on the 26th November 1648, the Christian Armies of Puritanism held a day-long prayer meeting during which they called upon God to guide them in their thoughts and actions. And God answered.

The King of England must die.

Poor Colonel Ashburnham came out of the sorry affair rather badly. There were accusations among the Royalists questioning the soundness of his judgement, of cowardice and even downright treachery. The king is said not to have believed Colonel John was unfaithful, although many still wonder; but the colonel was not the ghost of Carisbrooke Castle, nor was it the king. It was the Governor.

"I am trying to pierce a mist so strong. This place has changed much I fear. The King, the King! It was in the tiltyard I first walked with him. Oh, friend that I was. Hammond, my name, Governor of the Castle. I wish to pray, you came upon me suddenly. Allow me to present myself, Robert Hammond. It was here I sat and promised His Majesty I would help him as he wished to escape, but I went back on my oath.

I have been punished by roaming here through the centuries. I have followed wherever you went and I am very gratified that my likeness was in a drawing you found; not quite like me but being I suppose somewhat near what I may have looked like.

If one has taken an oath of allegiance, then that oath should be kept. In the room where I first spoke I oft sat as I used it for my accounts. My sin was to promise and then be a weak knave and turn my back on a man whom I liked; yet feared those in power. Always a man must stand up for what he believes or has promised, and not be swayed by others. Oh not to be chained to one place for eternity. I shall trouble you no more but hope I have not alarmed you nor the lady with you. I am going as if marching with a regiment of guards, with banners flying, muskets at shoulder. 'March onwards towards the light!' I hear the command. I obey. I obey."

*　　*　　*

Robert Hammond was Governor of the Isle of Wight for a mere two years, though arguably the Castle's most famous period. His next posting was as a Commissioner in Ireland, and there he died in October 1654.

CONCLUSION

The ghosts written about in these chapters are but a few of those who have spoken to me during what is now over twenty years of work. I do not have all the answers on the issue of ghosts and hauntings, but some matters seem obvious as a result of so much contact. Let me assure you, reader, ghosts do exist, and it is important you realise this.

The issue of the 'spirit body' or soul's existence is far from resolved, however much some might like to assume so and conclude the debate dead and buried. As the new millenium begins, those working at the leading-edge of science are now talking seriously of invisible universes and multi-dimensions, and even realms where space and time as we know them do not exist. As a consequence it looks likely that theories of the existence of the spirit body will have to be resurrected after all.

Generally most ghosts are nothing to be afraid of; some should not really be in that state at all and are more frightened than frightening, and if their presence can sometimes be felt it is usually only attempts to make contact and find help.

As already noted, after death there is a tunnel of light and those who do not go through it become earthbound. This can last for anything up to 500 years, as in the case of Margaret Pakenham (though one ghost removed from St Paul's cathedral in London had waited twice as long as that). As to why so many become earthbound, I can only tell you what the ghosts have told me. Some see the tunnel open and choose not to go through. This is a mistake, and when you, dear reader, find your time comes and the tunnel appears, take the opportunity and don't hang around to spook anyone before you go; for chances are the tunnel will close and you will be stuck.

Some prefer to stay in a familiar place rather than go through, some are too afraid to make the journey. However, the vast majority of ghosts are actually denied the passage of light; indeed many spirits have explained to me that they were told by females that they must stay in the scene of their crimes and reflect upon their misdeeds before going on for judgement. And strangely enough, this too seems to be administered by women. So I guess this raises Girl Power to heavenly levels . . .

APPENDIX

Beliefs that spirits of the dead can exist invisibly among the living were once common to the peoples of the earth, but are now dismissed as primitive – the product of a time when humans lacked discrimination and confused reality with the dreamlands experienced during sleep. Today these beliefs do remain in patches, but they are considered superstitious and heathen. In the jungles of South America, in the forests of Borneo and Africa; in the mountainous regions of Tibet and the frozen lands of northern Scandinavia, there are those who have always believed in unseen realms of existence and consider these to be as much a reality as our own, if not more so. To them spirits of the dead, or ghosts, are a fact. Only the body dies.

The religious traditions of the world originate from this belief and their history is the development of speculation over these "immaterial" dimensions – how they are peopled, who they are managed by, why and what their relationship is with our own; for the Afterlife has always had a powerful hold over the imagination.

Ever since it discarded the Heavenly Beings explanation some two and a half thousand years ago, Science has occasionally humoured the beliefs of the religious, but rarely embraced them. Science proclaims and concludes on the non-existence of the spirit or soul. In the absence of empirical evidence to the contrary this assertion stands; there is no "ghost in the machine" of the body to journey on. The body is all. When it dies so do you.

The implication is that those who entertain a belief in an Afterlife merely cling to the delusional, yet comforting, fantasy that there is more. Those who cannot come to terms with the terrible inevitability that the "me in here" will be no more; after all the pain and happiness, the lifetime of hard-earned experience and memories, for what? Nothing? So to compensate we invent the idea of an immortal soul to make us feel better about death.

Reluctance to entertain theories of an Afterlife and "immaterial" existence is understandable, for it is open to imaginative abuse and superstitious fancy. Instead Science steers toward that which can be identified and measured by the senses of the physical body. In contrast there is the unfounded conviction held by millions of humans, taught through many religions generation after generation, and advanced by the world's greatest thinkers from Pythagoras to Plato, that there is a soul and it does live on after death. This conviction alone does not prove its existence any more than the negative assertion of Science confirms its non-existence. Nevertheless, the belief there is more to life than simple termination remains – as unshakeable as it is unprovable.

No-one knows for sure of the existence of the Afterlife because no-one has come back with measurable proof; but some have come rather close and their experiences are worth more than the casual interest or indifferent dismissal that attend such testimonies. Modern medical technology has made it possible to bring back the dead. There are people who have been faced with the death of the body, the very moment, and tell us they had awareness, personal consciousness which did not cease when the body, technically, expired.

Such accounts are said to be mere hallucination induced by the disruption to the body's life support systems; that these hallucinations did in reality switch off when the body expired. What appeared to be continuation in consciousness was a delusion created by the mind to make sense of the temporary blip in operation while the body fluctuated between on and off, life and death. Without some empirical evidence, perhaps some kind of Heavenly Visa stamp, such accounts are bundled along with U.F.O. sightings, corn circles and other unexplainable phenomena to be filed under "Weird" or "X".

Yet there is consistency across the many case descriptions of the circumstances encountered during these important few moments – the brilliant light or tunnel, of drifting away from the physical body and toward the light; and many speak of hearing voices calling to them. As the cause and manifestation of each life-threatening situation is more or less unique, either the human species is pre-programmed with a 'Sweet Finale ' hallucination. Or the reason for this consistency of description is that what these people claim *is* true.

Of course the process cannot be verified empirically, for it is impossible to isolate a soul, take measurements and make tests as Science requires; or several minutes after the body is Flatline and beyond resuscitation call to the departing spirit, "Hey lady, what is it like to be on your way into another dimension? Talk me through it, eh? How about a quote?"

Perhaps it isn't so impossible after all.

SELECTED BIBLIOGRAPHY

Appledurcombe House. L. O. J. Boynton. English Heritage 1986.

A Ring of Magic Islands. Sybil and Stephen Leek. American Photographic Book Publishing Co. Inc. 1976.

A Royalist's Notebook. The Commonplace Book of Sir John Oglander, Kt, of Nunwell. Trans. Francis Bamford. Constable & Co. 1936.

Carisbrooke Castle. English Heritage 1985.

Isle of Wight Literary Haunts. Richard J. Hutchings. The Isle of Wight County Press 1989.

Letters Archæological and Historical Relating to the Isle of Wight. Rev. E. Boucher James. Frowde 1896.

The History of the Isle of Wight. Sir Richard Worsley. EP Publishing Ltd 1975.

The Life and Letters of John Keats. Lord Houghton. Everyman's Library.

The Architectural Antiquities of the Isle of Wight. Percy Goddard Stone 1891.

The Manor Houses of the Isle of Wight. C. W. R. Winter. Dovecote Press 1984.

The Mary Rose. The Excavation and Raising of Henry VIII's Flagship. Margaret Rule. Conway Maritime Press 1982.

The Oxford Illustrated History of English Literature. Ed. Pat Rogers. Oxford University Press 1987.

The Royal Prisoner. Jack D. Jones. Lutterworth Press 1965.

The Story of the Mary Rose. Ernle Bradford. Hamish Hamilton 1982.

Windsor Castle in the History of the Nation. A. L. Rowse. Book Club Associates 1974.